Reiner Schürmann
Selected Writings and Lecture Notes

T0366603

Reiner Schürmann

Reading Marx
On Transcendental Materialism

Lecture Notes for Courses at
the New School for Social Research

(Fall 1977)

Edited by
Malte Fabian Rauch and Nicolas Schneider

DIAPHANES

Reiner Schürmann
Selected Writings and Lecture Notes

Edited by Francesco Guercio, Michael Heitz,
Malte Fabian Rauch, and Nicolas Schneider

1st edition
ISBN 978-3-0358-0201-6
© DIAPHANES, Zurich 2021

Layout: 2edit, Zurich
Printed in Germany

www.diaphanes.com

Table of Contents

Syllabus

The starting point of this course is twofold: a) Marx's texts do not present a homogeneous doctrine; the most prominent example of that heterogeneity is the 'epistemological break' in 1845, but even after that break many lines of reflection, each of a different epistemological status, run parallel in his writings, b) the properly philosophical thread to follow is that of transcendental reflection upon the foundations of history, of social relations, and of economy. Hence the effort to 'read' Marx with a pre-understanding that is neither 'structuralist' nor 'humanist,' but one of transcendentalism.

List of Abbreviations

Schürmann quotes *The German Ideology*, the *Economic and Philosophic Manuscripts*, as well as *The Poverty of Philosophy* from Peter Furth and Hans-Joachim Lieber's German edition, and the English translation from a separate edition published by Progress Publishers. As the English translations are identical, references to this separate edition have been replaced with references to the *Marx/Engels Collected Works*. Since the *Marx-Engels-Werke* is still the most widely used German edition, references to this edition have been added.

Karl Marx and Friedrich Engels, *The German Ideology* (1845–1846)

DI   Karl Marx and Friedrich Engels, *Die Deutsche Ideologie*, in *Werke–Schriften*, vol. 2, *Frühe Schriften*, eds. Hans-Joachim Lieber and Peter Furth (Darmstadt: Wissenschaftliche Buchgesellschaft, 1971), 5–655.

MEW 3   Karl Marx and Friedrich Engels, *Die Deutsche Ideologie*, in *Marx-Engels-Werke*, vol. 3 (Berlin: Dietz Verlag, 1978), 9–438.

MECW 5   Karl Marx and Friedrich Engels, *The German Ideology*, in *Marx/Engels Collected Works*, vol. 5 (Moscow: Progress Publishers, 1975), 19–452.

Karl Marx, *Economic and Philosophic Manuscripts* (1844)

MS   Karl Marx, *Ökonomisch-Philosophische Manuskripte*, in *Werke–Schriften*, vol. 1, *Frühe Schriften*, eds. Hans-Joachim Lieber and Peter Furth (Darmstadt: Wissenschaftliche Buchgesellschaft, 1971), 506–665.

MEW 40   Karl Marx and Friedrich Engels, *Ökonomisch-Philosophische Manuskripte aus dem Jahre 1844*, in *Marx-Engels-Werke*, vol. 40 (Berlin: Dietz Verlag, 1968), 465–588.

MECW 3   Karl Marx and Friedrich Engels, *Economic and Philosophic Manuscripts of 1844*, trans. Martin Milligan and Dirk J. Struik, in *Marx/Engels Collected Works*, vol. 3 (London: Lawrence and Wishart, 1975), 229–357.

Karl Marx, *The Poverty of Philosophy* (1847)

EP   Karl Marx, *Das Elend der Philosophie*, in *Werke–Schriften*, vol. 2, *Frühe Schriften*, eds. Hans-Joachim Lieber and Peter Furth (Darmstadt: Wissenschaftliche Buchgesellschaft, 1971), 657–811.

MEW 4   Karl Marx, *Das Elend der Philosophie*, in *Marx-Engels-Werke*, vol. 4 (Berlin: Dietz Verlag, 1977), 63–182.

MECW 6 Karl Marx, *The Poverty of Philosophy*, in *Marx/Engels Collected Works*, vol. 6 (London: Lawrence & Wishart, 1976), 105–212.

Karl Marx, *Critique of Hegel's Philosophy of Right* (1843–1844)

Karl Marx wrote two separate texts that were to constitute the *Kritik der Hegelschen Rechtsphilosophie*: first, the *Kritik des Hegelschen Staatsrechts* (§§261–313), printed in *MEW* 1, 203–333; second, the *Kritik der Hegelschen Rechtsphilosophie: Einleitung*, printed in *MEW* 1, 378–391. The English translation in *Marx/Engels Collected Works* refers to the first text as *Contribution to the Critique of Hegel's Philosophy of Law*, *MECW* 3, 3–129; the second text is rendered as *A Contribution to the Critique of Hegel's Philosophy of Law: Introduction*, printed in *MECW* 3, 175–187. The Bottomore edition, which Schürmann uses, contains an excerpt from Marx's *Introduction*.

CHR   Karl Marx, *Selected Writings in Sociology & Social Philosophy*, trans. and ed. Tom B. Bottomore (New York: McGraw-Hill, 1964), 179–183.

MEW 1   Karl Marx, *Kritik der Hegelschen Rechtsphilosophie [Kritik des Hegelschen Staatsrechts (§§261–313)]; Kritik der Hegelschen Rechtsphilosophie: Einleitung*, in *Marx-Engels-Werke*, vol. 1 (Berlin: Dietz Verlag, 1981), 201–333; 378–391.

MECW 3 Karl Marx, *Contribution to the Critique of Hegel's Philosophy of Law; A Contribution to the Critique of Hegel's Philosophy of Law: Introduction*, in *Marx/Engels Collected Works*, vol. 6 (London: Lawrence & Wishart, 1976), 3–129; 175–187.

Karl Marx, *Theses on Feuerbach* (1845)

TF   Karl Marx, *Selected Writings in Sociology & Social Philosophy*, trans. and
ed. Tom B. Bottomore (New York: McGraw-Hill, 1964), 67–69.

MEW 3   Karl Marx, *Thesen über Feuerbach*, in *Marx-Engels-Werke*, vol. 3 (Berlin: Dietz Verlag, 1978), 5–7.

MECW 5 Karl Marx, *Theses on Feuerbach*, in *Marx/Engels Collected Works*,
vol. 5 (Moscow: Progress Publishers, 1975), 3–5.

Michel Henry, *Marx*

Throughout the lecture, Schürmann refers to Michel Henry's two volume study
Marx with a typed abbreviation in the left margin of his script. In the present
edition, references to the French original and the English translation are placed
in parentheses in the text body, following Schürmann's placement as closely
as possible. The Roman numerical after *H* refers to the volume number of the
French edition, followed by the page number. Wherever possible, page references to the English translation are given after the slash. Frequently, however,
Schürmann refers to passages not included in the English translation.

H I   Michel Henry, *Marx*, vol. 1, *Une philosophie de la réalité* (Paris: Gallimard, 1976).

H II   Michel Henry, *Marx*, vol. 2, *Une philosophie de l'économie* (Paris: Gallimard, 1976).

In collaboration with Henry, an abridged translation of both volumes was published as *Marx: A Philosophy of Human Reality*, trans. Kathleen Blamey McLaughlin (Bloomington: Indiana University Press, 1983).

For other texts by Marx and Engels that Schürmann refers to less frequently,
references to the most accessible German and English editions are given with the
following abbreviations, followed by the volume number:

MEW   Karl Marx and Friedrich Engels, *Marx-Engels-Werke*, 44 vols. (Berlin: Dietz Verlag, 1956–).

MECW   Karl Marx and Friedrich Engels, *Collected Works*, 50 vols. (London
and New York: Lawrence & Wishart, 1975–).

11

Introduction:
Marx as Transcendental Philosopher

The title that I have chosen for this course is, of course, inspired by
Althusser (*Reading Capital*)—but polemically so. By 'reading Marx'
I mean: reading Karl Marx and not Engels, Mao, Gramsci, Lukács,
Marcuse, Althusser et al. In other words: the goal of the course is,
first of all, to deliberately disentangle Marx's thinking from Marxist
thinking. An implicit polemic with some Marxists will be carried
out backstage, i.e., by occasional suggestions.

Such a program vehicles three major implications: a) that there
is indeed a difference in thinking between Marx and Marxism. This
first point will be established through a philosophical reading of
Marx: the assumption is that what is most original in Marx is neither his political thinking nor his sociological or economic¹ thinking, but his philosophical axis. This philosophical axis determines
and localizes his other theories. b) The second implication in the
separation between Marx and Marxism is that Marxism as such
exists, can be characterized by general features, and that these
general features differ from Marx's original thinking or restrict it
(*H* I, 9/1). This is a very complex and complicated matter; but let
me summarize this cleavage by saying that Marxism has retained
from Marx primarily the elements that serve political action in a
given, pressing, situation. A theory of "revolutionary practice"
has thus taken the place of philosophy. c) The third implication
concerns the pre-understanding in approaching the texts. A text is
something printed: as such it is closed, constituted, finished. But
we shall obtain decisive answers from it only if we raise decisive
questions. The decisive question raised by Marxists is the urgency
of a revolutionary situation (either existing in fact or to be brought
about). Thus their question is generally similar to Lenin's *What
is to be Done?*. It is the question of those whom Althusser calls
the "militant intellectuals" who participate directly in the struggle
of the working class.² Such a 'reading' of Marx is strategic. I say
that the strategic reading remains, by its very nature, blind to the

philosophical question. Thus our pre-understanding of Marx's texts is not strategic, but rather that they yield an answer to the oldest question in Western philosophy: *ti to on*; or, What is being?, What is reality? and the corollary: What is truth?[3]

So: Marx vs Marxism: the concept of 'praxis' as the differential concept between Marx and Marxism; a two-fold theory of texts. Let me develop these three points a little farther.

a) Marx versus Marxism

This distinction has been made frequently. The way I am going to handle it results from the basic orientation of this course. Whereas I characterize Marxism primarily as a theory of action, I plan to treat Marx as a transcendental philosopher developing the foundations of history, of social relations, and of economy, out of a theory of the subject.[4] To make it brief, the thesis is that Marx's answer to the question "What is man?"[5] is: the laboring individual, and that historicization and structuralization to be understood in their essence have to be reduced to this foundation in individual practice.

Thus I take the exact counter-position to what is, for instance, spelled out in the first lines of the article 'Marxist Philosophy' in the *Encyclopedia of Philosophy*: "Marx did not write a philosophy and would have regarded 'Marxist philosophy' as a contradiction in terms; he considered his work to be scientific, historical, and sociological, as opposed to 'philosophical' divagations."[6] This is totally mistaken at least for the texts of the middle period, after 1845, *The German Ideology* and even *The Poverty of Philosophy*. What Marx polemically criticizes as 'philosophy' in these texts is a particular way of philosophizing—precisely that way of philosophizing that does not reduce reality to its foundations in individual practice, but rather to consciousness. Only if 'philosophy' means 'philosophy of consciousness' would Marxian philosophy be indeed a contradiction in terms.

The philosophical axis that determines and localizes Marx's theories of history, of social relations and of economy, will have to be worked out from the texts. If it is true that this philosophical axis is of the transcendental type, then Marx's philosophizing

14

will itself be located within a particular realm of doing philosophy. This realm is not the realm of so-called 'epistemological structuralism' for which philosophy is a type of practice, comparable to scientific practice, both being aimed at 'intervention' in social life ("the political character of my philosophical essays").[7] Nor is that transcendental realm the realm of so-called 'humanistic' Marxism, be it of the disciples of Horkheimer and Adorno or the members of the circle around the Yugoslav periodical *Praxis* (Petrovich, Markovich, Stejanovich),[8] since it is precisely not aimed at the resolution of alienation, at the liberation of man, or the critique of late capitalism.[9] These two schools, indeed, are schools of Marxism. Marxian transcendentalism is something different. This difference can be observed already simply by enumerating the basic concepts of Marxism, compared to the basic concepts of *The German Ideology*:[10] class-struggle, alienation, dialectical materialism etc. vs the insistence, on nearly every page of *The German Ideology*, on the working individual, i.e., on the subjectivity of (social, political, and economic) forces.

It will appear that the Marxist reading of Marx locates these forces, or the classes, at the beginning of the analysis, whereas the productive forces and the classes are seen by Marx as grounded in individual practice which alone gives them their value and explains the capitalist system (*H* I, 30/14). A transcendental argument reasons from the empirical to its grounding in subjectivity. This grounding is more certain than the empirical that appears. Marx's unique place in the history of philosophy stems from the fact that such grounding of phenomena is seen by him not as a relation that produces cognition, as in Kant; nor as a relation of material sensitivity, as in Feuerbach; but the grounding occurs in labor, in practice, in the satisfaction of needs. The Marxist reading of Marx reverses this order of foundation: instead of grounding the classes and the productive forces on the individual practice, it sees these classes and forces as primary realities. For Marx, on the contrary, they are what has to be explained, not that which explains.

The opposition 'Marx vs Marxism' is thus articulated here as an opposition between an understanding of being vs theories of action. Marx's understanding of man is transcendental, since reality is discovered in individual practice, i.e., in production, and since this individual practice founds history, social formations, and economics (*H* I, 29/13–14).[11]

The so-called 'humanist' Marxists whom I have mentioned suggest this foundation sometimes, e.g. Marcuse, *Reason and Revolution*.[12] But they necessarily cover up transcendental subjectivity by a moral interest. (See the usage, for instance, that Marcuse makes of the quote from *The German Ideology*, "Each Man has a particular, exclusive sphere of activity, which is forced upon him and from which he cannot escape" (*MEW* 3, 33/*MECW* 5, 47).[13] Marcuse sees there an indication that: "The individuals are isolated from and set against each other," an indication of the "alienation of man from man," whereas that line from *The German Ideology* is meant to indicate the origin of the division of labor in the sphere of an individual's activity!).

The transcendental line of Marx interpretation has been developed further by Hans Staudinger here at the New School,[14] by Michel Henry,[15] and by Kostas Axelos,[16] and the periodical *Arguments* (1956–1962).[17]

b) The differentiating concept of practice

At first sight, there seems to be a continuity between Marx as a transcendental philosopher the way it has been outlined, and Marxism. Indeed, both ways of thinking center around a certain understanding of practice. Let me repeat these two concepts of practice: for Marx, practice is what in *The German Ideology* he calls 'reality' and 'life,' always predicated of the individual. In other words this concept designates the concrete mode of satisfying basic human needs. The way one satisfies one's hunger, need for shelter, and some other things of that order—i.e., 'praxis.' For the Marxists, practice is bound up with social configurations. Let me begin with this second notion of practice.

Here again, Marxists of the two extremes agree on the priority—ontological priority, as we shall see—of constituted wholes[18] over the individual, be these wholes classes, the civil society altogether, or the state. The key concepts of the two most prominent Marxist schools today indicate this social essence of practice. On the side of the 'humanist' Marxists: what is the best-known concept of the best-known theoretician, Marcuse, here? The 'Great Refusal.' Such refusal is assuredly something practical. The concept is borrowed from Whitehead, but Marcuse defines it as the "protest against unnecessary repression" and as "the ultimate form of freedom."[19] The middle term that ties the Great Refusal to social practice is, in Marcuse, the libido: "The Orphic-Narcissistic images are those of the Great Refusal: refusal to accept separation from the libidinous object (or subject)."[20] But immediately we are told that as "an isolated individual phenomenon, the reactivation of narcissistic libido is not culture-binding but neurotic [...] Libido can take the road of self-sublimation only as a *social* phenomenon [...]."[21] The goal is to render the "reactivation of polymorphous and narcissistic sexuality" culture-binding.[22] Even in the face of death the "great refusal" is a social practice.[23]

At the other extreme of the Marxist spectrum—again, only to take the best known theoreticians—'practice' is the key concept, too: "By *practice* in general I shall mean any process of *transformation* of determinate given raw material into a determinate *product*, a transformation effected by a determinate human labor, using determinate means (of 'production')."[24] This definition encompasses many different types of practice: economic (production, circulation, consumption), theoretical (philosophy and science), political, and ideological (art, culture in general). In each of these practices Althusser distinguishes between the raw material, the labor force, the means of production and the product. The purpose of the wide range of acceptations of the concept of practice is precisely to make practice coextensive with life. Here again, then, we are indeed faithful to Marx. But how is practice, so defined, coextensive with life? By the resolution of such classical antinomies as 'theory and practice,' 'individual and public,' under the one concept of practice, so that we have "economic practice," "theoretical practice," "political practice," "ideological practice."[25] Practice, in this sense, is never individual practice. Althusser puts it briefly: "philosophy, in the last resort, is the class struggle in theory."[26] Practice is the class struggle. It is the class struggle that is found in all domains: economic, theoretical, political, ideological.

Something totally different is at stake in the philosophical writings of Marx. I have said that, beginning with *The German Ideology*, practice is subjective need (*H* I, 294/123).[27] Need of appropriation and incorporation of things exterior to the self. What Marx calls 'reality' is the relation of exteriority between the self and the object of its need. 'Praxis' means the moving subjectivity of a concrete individual (*H* I, 356). 'Praxis' is nothing but the elementary activity of men 'making a living' or busy with living (*H* I, 357). In commenting from this particular aspect of ontology on the *Theses on Feuerbach*, we shall see later that they all develop, one after the other, the equation between *praxis* and *being* (*H* I, 316/139). This is the radical novelty in Marx. And to isolate for instance the eleventh of these *Theses* ("The philosophers have only interpreted the world in different ways; the point is to change it") as if it contained a program for action is to completely misunderstand the tenor of it. This eleventh thesis is an abridgment of Marx's ontology of practice and as such unintelligible when merely taken by itself. The *Theses on Feuerbach* refute an ontology based on entities conceived by the mind or by consciousness—entities such as 'class,' 'human species,' 'state' etc. (*H* I, 319/141). In a sense it is the realism of universals—which Marxism hastens to restore—that these *Theses* refute (*H* I, 357–358). The Marxist "social practice" still deals with such universals: society at large, the 'whole,' 'man,' 'History,' the 'structure' of an epistemological field. But 'the' praxis, or with a capital 'P,' does not exist for Marx. There are only individual satisfactions of needs. The great hypostases, Social Practice, the Movement of Society, the March of History etc., still locate 'praxis' in the general. This notion of individual practice as the origin of economics, theory, politics and all forms of ideology is the great discovery of the Spring of 1845—a discovery so violent that it translates itself into the ferocious and unending polemics of *The German Ideology* and *The Poverty of Philosophy*.

The concept of 'practice' is the differentiating concept between Marx and the Marxists since it indicates best the equivocity of an ontology of universals and an ontology based on the individual effort to live.

c) The theory of texts[28]

From the remarks just made it results that Marx's writings are not homogenous. There are several breaks in his writings. The main break occurs in the Spring of 1845. Althusser says that "the frontier separating ideology from scientific theory was crossed about one hundred and twenty years ago by Marx." He excludes any continuity whatsoever between the young Marx and the middle period. In fact, already in the early writings one can detect the problematic that I called transcendentalism of individual practice. Althusser's option for Marxism over ‹ and › against Marx makes himself go as far as to say: "the application of Marxist theory to Marx himself appears to be the absolute precondition of an understanding of Marx [...]."[29]

On the contrary, in the writings before 1845 one has to distinguish a double problematic: a minor problematic and a major problematic. The major problematic in the early writings of Marx is what I called the realism of universals, i.e., of the 'generic being,' 'man,' 'society,' 'history' et al. (*H* I, 184/86–87). The decisive conceptual mutation that occurs in the Spring of 1845 pushes this problematic into the background; it reappears, however, even in later writings. What comes to the fore is the minor problematic until 1845, already present in the manuscript of 1842–1843 *Critique of Hegel's Philosophy of the State* [*Kritik des Hegelschen Staatsrechts*]:[30] the realism of the concrete individual. The mutation of 1845 rests on ultimate ontological assumptions, namely: it is no longer (as for the tradition out of which he grew) the ideal universality of objectivity which defines reality. From 1845 on, neither 'man' as a universal, nor 'society,' nor 'history' "exist" properly speaking. They are merely words, from now on—and in that sense Marx's ontology of the concrete individual belongs to the tradition of nominalism. So much so that in *The Poverty of Philosophy* Marx borrows the following expressions from an American economist: "The moral entity—the grammatical being called a nation, has been clothed in attributes that have no real existence except in the imagination of those who metamorphose a word into a thing" (*EP*, 725/*MECW* 6, 153/*MEW* 4, 115).[31]

The so-called epistemological break of 1845 is thus the reversal of a relation between two problematics of realism:

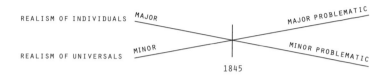

This reversal can be summarized as a refusal of the concept of society as a person: *"the person, Society"*[32] in which "relations are not relations between individual and individual, but between worker and capitalist, between farmer and landlord etc." does not exist (*EP*, 725/*MECW* 6, 152, 159/*MEW* 4, 115, 123; *H* I, 188/89). This 'break' is with any concept hypostatized; with any entity that would transcend the individual and dominate it. It is a break with the philosophy of man as philosophy of the universal and its categories.[33] "Man," with a capital "M," does not exist for Marx—nor do the classes, as autonomous entities. They do not precede the individual ontologically: that is the discovery of 1845.

The theory of texts that I am developing rests on three principles:

1. Marx's writings are heterogeneous: the most decisive break occurs in 1845, but there are other breaks between the writings with economic, philosophical, political or ideological problematics.

2. The key concepts of Marxism are developed from the political texts, that is: *The Communist Manifesto*, *The Eighteenth Brumaire of Louis Bonaparte*, *The Class Struggles in France* etc. (*H* I, 10/2).[34] But these texts do not carry their principle of intelligibility in themselves, since they are chiefly historical works.

3. The key concepts of Marx's philosophy must be developed from the first work after the break of 1845, i.e., *The German Ideology*. It then appears that these concepts enter an old debate of what is being.

These three principles are formulated against both Althusser and Marcuse: It is not a new 'science' that the break inaugurates, but an ontology (i.e., vs Althusser). And: this break by no means implies the negation of philosophy (i.e., vs Marcuse):

> The transition from Hegel to Marx is, in all respects, a transition to an essentially different order of truth, not to be interpreted in terms of philosophy. We shall see that all the philosophical concepts of Marxian theory are social and economic categories, whereas Hegel's social and economic categories are all philosophical concepts. Even Marx's early writings are not philosophical. They express the negation of philosophy, though they still do so in philosophical language.[35] (*H* I, 15/5)

Thus there are chiefly text-immanent reasons for the reading of Marx that I am going to suggest. There is also an extrinsic reason, since I read him in the framework of Heideggerian "Destruction of the History of Ontology." In this perspective, precisely, Marx belongs to the tradition of transcendental subjectivity. Within the 'field' or 'epoch' of transcendentalism Marx occupies this eminent place of an entirely new concept of the transcendental ego. The transcendental ego is not the knowing subject, but the laboring subject. This puts indeed an end to one type of philosophy, but at the same time such a transcendentalism belongs to the very core of the Western philosophical tradition. It is one answer to the 'question of being.'

Transcendental philosophy thus undergoes its decisive mutation in Marx. At the beginning of the 'epoch' of transcendentalism, in Kant, the term 'transcendental' is defined by the famous passage from the *Critique of Pure Reason*: "I entitle 'transcendental' all knowledge which is occupied not so much with objects as with the mode of our knowledge of objects in so far as this mode of knowledge is to be possible 'a priori'" (B25).[36] Although, even in Kant, there are other meanings to the term 'transcendental,' it is safe to say that they all refer to an a priori constitution of knowledge—even in the practical philosophy: there it is the a priori constitution of the moral ought, and the way it imposes itself on action (through maxims!), which is called transcendental. It is this epistemological status of the transcendental ego that Marx destroys. The a priori is not a matter of reason, be it pure or practical, but labor, need, practice. In reading Marx we entitle 'transcendental' not a knowledge, but concrete, individual action. However, we remain in the mainstream of transcendentalism when we see Marx developing the foundation of economics, politics and ideologies out of their rootedness in the producing individual.

It is true that Heidegger himself has not developed this phenomenological destruction of Marx's ontology. There are only nine allusions to Marx in Heidegger's works.[37] But the Heideggerian presuppositions coincide here with the basic turn of the decisive philosophical texts after 1845.

A Double Problematic in the Early Writings

To read Marx as a transcendental philosopher means four things: to trace phenomena (of history, politics, economics) back to their condition in subjectivity; to understand subjectivity not as that of the knowing, but that of the acting individual; to see all constituted wholes (classes, the state) as derived from individual practice; to understand practice as the originary site of truth. Before tracing the double problematic in the early writings, let me develop this last point, the theory of foundation of truth more in detail.

1. The originary site of truth

Transcendental philosophy claims to be able to found truth—that is, exhibit the structures which are indubitable in so far as they make truth possible (*H* I, 477/187). These structures are those of the subject. In turning to them, instead of universals, in our quest for certainty, we actually do two things: we discover the locus, the 'site' where truth arises (literally: its 'origin,' *oriri*), where it is 'at home,' i.e., its site of competence. The site of competence of truth, according to Marx, is the laboring individual. The second thing we do in turning towards the structures of subjectivity, is to recognize a ground on which all other determinations rest; a ground that is reliable, since it produces knowledge, and a ground that is permanent, since it is made of formal structures. Transcendental subjectivity, in that sense, is a system of forms—in Marx, a system of forms of production.

The recognition, by Marx, of the laboring individual as the originary site of truth takes on, first of all, the form of a critique: the critique of any ideality insofar as it pretends to found truth; the critique of any ideal truth to be self-sufficient or autonomous. In *The German Ideology* Marx calls this originary site of truth 'reality,' 'life.' This means that he criticizes idealities in as much as they are held to constitute truth by themselves, deprived of any reference to such 'reality,' 'life.' If reality, understood as the laboring individual, is to ground all other determinations—the different types of 'practice' that I mentioned in Althusser—then the laboring individual is a 'principle,' that which is *primum captum,* grasped first of all, caught sight of first of all. This is the strong sense of Marx's transcendentalism: the individual in its need and its effort to satisfy its need, is the principle of history, politics and economy. This is the genuine sense of historical materialism, as we shall see, in Marx: 'materialism' means the explanation of phenomena by the needs and their satisfaction which underlie them; and 'historical' in so far as such materialism is opposed to an 'ideal materialism' such as Feuerbach's. I already indicated that Marx's notion of 'history' is understandable only in relation to the laboring individual. 'Historical materialism' does not mean: economic, theoretical, political and ideological practices are rooted in the modes of production of a given period, so that in a feudalistic society the mode of production leads to other kinds of economics, other ideas etc. than an urban society, or an industrial society. This is of course true, but such is Marx's thinking in his historical writings. This kind of determination by labor is operative in his historiography. The strict sense of the concept of 'historical materialism' lies elsewhere: whatever may be the models of producing, circulating, consuming, philosophizing, painting etc., these modes are always grounded, they have their site of truth, in the laboring individual. The adjective 'historical' in the title 'historical materialism' thus refers to history not as factual history (duration, years and centuries), but to 'history' as another name for individual practice, i.e., transcendental history.

In this sense alone is the term 'historical materialism' justified: it is the theory of all possible theories (*H* I, 478/188). Or again: it is practice, in as much as it is subjective, which founds factual history and a theory of factual history. It may seem that with Marx's transcendentalism truth simply changes its site: from ideality to practice; but the change is more radical: the displacement from ideality into practice modifies the nature of truth itself. Truth is no longer a representation of consciousness. Neither consciousness, nor knowledge, nor theory can claim to constitute truth. Truth is constituted by Marx through the satisfaction of individual needs. This shift from a philosophy of consciousness to one of the practical satisfaction of needs, I have said, occurs in the Spring of 1845. However, before this 'break,' the new theme announces itself already. I now have to show briefly how in the writings before 1845 the double problematic—truth as representation and truth as practice—is already present.

2. The twofold concept of 'civil society' in the early writings[38]

I shall refer here to Marx's critique of Hegel's philosophy of right (1842–1843).[39] From these texts I only take the elements that allow understanding the ambiguity in Marx's notion of civil society at that period, since the twofold problematic is precisely located on that level. To summarize what I have to say: "In Hegel, the real subjects [...] become objective moments of the idea, not real" (*MEW* 1, 206/ *MECW* 3, 8; *H* I, 39/20).[40] Marx's objection to Hegel here consists in saying: Hegel describes the interplay of individual activity on the level of civil society not for itself, not as the originary site of reality, but for the sake of the 'law' of the idea. Hegel thus is not interested in the autonomy of the reality of individual interchange. Marx's critique is a critique of all subsumption of the particular under the universal—but at the same time, still in Hegelian vocabulary, hence the twofold notion of 'civil society.'

The '*Bürger*,' in this context, is not the citizen, *Staatsbürger*, but the private individual in so far as "it has its proper interest as its goal."[41] Hegel called this individual the '*Konkretum*,' or the 'bourgeois': thus he analyses social relations twice, once as the 'civil' network of satisfactions of interest and need, and once as those of the 'citizen,' *citoyen*. Thus at first sight, Hegel fully recognizes not only the individual's rights, but also its transcendental status: the civil society is altogether built on the autonomy of the individual. But then what happens? After having clearly separated the realm of the individual, i.e., civil society, from the realm of the citizen, i.e., the state, Hegel develops a series of mediations from one to the other. Marx's critique, in these early texts, hinges entirely on the role of these mediations. Indeed, what is meant by 'mediation' (*H* I, 59/35)?

The presupposition of Hegel's quest for mediations between the civil society and the state, Marx argues, is the real heterogeneity of individual and state—as if the state, a universal, were an in-itself opposable to the individual. And the function of the mediations will show that Hegel's concept of the civil society, despite its first appearance, is already one of a universal. But Marx's starting point is clear: if you speak of mediations between the individual laboring to satisfy its needs, and the state, the two enter into the arena as 'persons.' We have the "person, the individual," and, "the person, the State." As I already suggested, in *The Poverty of Philosophy* the first of these two persons is clearly addressed as "the person, Society": this latter title, in Marx's reading of Hegel, is actually the proper title for the individual in civil society. The recognition of the individual's autonomy is only a 'moment' for Hegel, before it is subsumed under a universal. The four mediations that follow only operate such subsumption.

a) The first and most important mediation, established by Hegel between the civil society and the state, are the estates. The estates, in the sense of the Middle Ages, are supposed to mediate between private interest and the general interest. "The *estates* are *the posited contradiction* between the State and the civil society within the State; at the same time they are the *claim* to *solve* this contradiction" (*MEW* 1, 270/*MECW* 3, 67).[42] Thus to conceive the estates as mediating between individual fulfillment of needs and the general interest is precisely to hypostatize the general ‹ as › an in-itself: otherwise there could be no "posited contradiction."[43] This is, of course, abbreviating the analysis that Hegel gives: but that much is clear: the estates are the locus where the universal contradicts the individual; where the goals of the State clash with the goals of the individual. Hegel thought that the passage from civil society to the political society could be based on an ontology of the universal (*H* I, 61/37); but the consequence of his position was that the civil society itself ended up subsumed under the universal—hence the well-known universals that make up the civil society: family, corporations, etc. In the individual the conflict of private and public opens a "double life":[44] on the one hand, he is the 'real' man pursuing the satisfaction of his need, on the other he is part of a universal, a citizen.

b) The civil servants (*H* I, 64/39). Here it is the bureaucracy that establishes the mediation between the civil society and the State (in the form of the government).

c) The critique of economics. In this manuscript, it is particularly primogeniture and landed property that appear as a mediation between private and public interest. Indeed, landed property appears as the triumph of the universal over the individual. According to Hegel, Marx writes, property is supposed to express the free will, to realize rationally and spiritually the freedom of the will. But landed property means the exact opposite of such independence, since the entire social order depends on it. Property, Marx writes, is thus turned into an absolute: "my will does not possess, it is possessed" (*MEW* 1, 306/*MECW* 3, 101). "Private property has become the subject of will, and will is only the predicate of private property" (*MEW* 1, 305/*MECW* 3, 100). So, the view on economics—before Marx actually undertook economic studies—again exhibits the universal at work in private property. Private property becomes even the determinant of the universal, the State: "the political constitution in its highest expression is the constitution of private property" (*MEW* 1, 303/*MECW* 3, 98).

d) Elections. Here more clearly than anywhere else, the individual is identified with the member of the State (*H* I, 74/47). Thus the universal is posited right away as the essence of the individual. The mediation of elections was meant to answer, in Hegel, the dilemma: either all participate in the affairs of the State, but that is impossible, or only some: these are the delegates. Marx's objection is: the individual is not to be seen as part of the State, but the State is the individual's part (*Anteil*) (*MEW* 1, 323/*MECW* 3, 116). "Not all participate in it individually, but the individuals in as much as they are all" (*MEW* 1, 322/*MECW* 3, 116; *H* I, 74/47). This formulation wants to destroy the Hegelian illusion that the individual is originally separated from the universal and must then, by a mediation, be reconciled with it.

But here you also see in what sense Marx does remain Hegelian in this early text: Both when all participate, he says, and when only the delegates participate in the business of the State, "the universal simply remains outside the individual as an exterior plurality or totality. [In that case, i.e., in Hegel—R.S.] the universal is not an essential, spiritual, real quality of the individual" (*MEW* 1, 322/ *MECW* 3, 117).

Thus the goal of the critique of the mediations is to interiorize the universal in the individual. Marx challenges a concept of the individual which would not define it by "its universal and objective qualities" (*H* I, 76/48). This 'universal and objective quality,' although placed in the individual from the outset (and not by mediation) is evidently again the hypostasis of a universal, in Marx... The hypostasis which Marx had precisely denounced in Hegel. This is expressed in our text: in the civil society "each individual acts for the others and all others act for him" (*H* I, 77/50). The universal is thus again analytically included in the reality of the acting individual. Every need is thus determined by the relational totality, the reciprocity with the others. Now, what is posited at the outset by Marx is no longer the individual, but the essence, the universal, or, in Feuerbach's terms, 'man' (*H* I, 82/51). This remains, despite the appearance of the individual as ultimate foundation, the major problematic in the manuscript of 1842.

3. The critique of alienations in the early writings

The same double problematic can be observed in Marx's critique of alienation in the early writings. The ambiguity stems from the fact that Marx chooses the vocabulary of Feuerbach to oppose the realism of universals in Hegel—'generic being,' 'man,' 'matter.' But all these terms are again only a transformed Hegelianism. Still they contain the very elements that will overthrow Hegelianism in 1845. This potential of a new understanding of being is what I want to show—not the critique of alienations itself.[45]

To anticipate the conclusion: alienation will be seen a) as the separation of the individual from what is properly human in him, i.e., universal, 'man'; in this line of thought the task consists in "making everyone aware that they belong to the same species or collectivity" (*H* II, 11);[46] b) as the separation of the individual from himself: the individual appears as split, half private half public; in this line of thought the task is to affirm the qualities of 'spirituality,' 'human dignity,' etc. for the defense of the individual. This is particularly transparent in the article "On Lumber Theft":[47] the general interest is defined in reference to the many individuals that compose it.

a) The generic being as fulfillment of the individual. The clearest example of alienation is religion. Religious man displaces what is properly human in him; in the language borrowed from Feuerbach:[48] he projects his generic being into an unattainable heaven. In other words, religion is the most visible case of representation: man's genuine qualities are 'rendered present again' on another level, out-side of himself. To re-appropriate man's generic being can become the task only on a twofold condition: that his generic being be so displaced; and that this displacement be a matter of conscious-ness (H I, 87). It is by the same movement of thought that man becomes consciousness, and religion a representation. This double turn yields an understanding of being where 'reality' is placed in the autonomy of consciousness insofar as consciousness is able to appropriate its own '*Gattungswesen.*' The resolution of alienation, too, points to this ontology of universals, the realism of universals: the appropriation of man's being consists in rejecting his represen-tations, criticized as such. You recognize Feuerbach's program of reducing theology to anthropology. "Religion is only the illusory sun that circles around man as long as he does not circle around himself" (*MEW* 1, 379/*MECW* 3, 176). Here, and elsewhere, Marx does not say 'consciousness,' but 'man.' But the slogan: "give back to man what belongs to him," as it originates in the critique of reli-gion, is clearly aimed at a re-appropriation through consciousness. Man, 'consciousness,' 'generic being' all indicate the universal that Feuerbach describes as made of intelligence, sensibility, love, free disposition etc. In religion all these qualities have been attributed to God, whereas they are properly human qualities. Their place of origin is in man, and the divine predicates must become human properties again.

But these human faculties are meant precisely to define man as such, his 'essence,' i.e., man universally (H I, 91). Marx wants to carry out what he calls a "radical critique": "To be radical is to take things at their root. Now, for man the root is man himself" (*MEW* 1, 385/*MECW* 3, 182). In other words, the root of the individual is man as a universal. The individual is not its own foundation. Its foun-dation is the human species, which gathers together the infinite number of predicates that define man, and of which an individual can only claim a few (*H* I, 93). The species is infinite, but the individual is finite. You are familiar with this theme—but its implication should be clear: if the species, or the generic being, is the sum total of all human qualities, it falls itself under the critique of representation. The critique of religion as man's alienation had precisely set off from the separation of man from his essential qualities. This separation was to be overcome. But the radical critique perpetuates the same separation in simply another vocabulary: the human species, or generic being, contains all qualities—and the individual only some. One has to say of the 'generic being,' 'Man,' what Marx says of religion: "Gods are *originally* not the cause but the effect of man's intellectual confusion" (*MS*, 572/*MEW* 40, 520/ *MECW* 3, 279–280).

The same argument could be carried out with regard to the famous reconciliation between man and nature, "nature perfectly humanized and man perfectly naturalized." Indeed, in the ‹ *Economic and Philosophic* › *Manuscripts* of 1844, the relation between man and nature is precisely the content of the concept of 'generic being' (*H* I, 103/54). Marx gives the example of sexuality: i.e., not a relation of individuals, but a generic relation (*MS*, 592/*MEW* 40, 535/*MECW* 3, 295–296).—This realism of the universals 'Man,' 'generic being' etc. is the major problematic in the early writings.

b) The generic being as alienation of the individual. This is the exact counter-proposition to the previous one; it constitutes the minor problematic in the early writings. The point here is to understand, as I suggested, the generic being as pertaining to the public realm, dividing the individual with himself. And Marx will say: the essential qualities must be realized in the individual himself; it is not enough to claim them by a 'theology' turned into 'anthropology' (*H* I, 88). It is not enough to overturn the schemes of consciousness. From the divine to the human, we still move within modifications of consciousness. But Marx asks: How does consciousness produce, at one time, the schemes of religion, and at another time the anthropological schemes which are critical of religion? Stated otherwise: How is Feuerbach's rearrangement of the Hegelian universalism possible? "It is possible because self-consciousness is the creative principle of religious representations, but as a consciousness that has become exterior to itself, alienated from and dispossessed of itself. When self-consciousness has recovered itself, grasped its own essence, it becomes the force that rules over the creations of its self-alienation."[49] The tone of these lines is polemic: Marx wants to say that dispossession and repossession of consciousness remain unexplained. Thus he locates himself outside of the entire problematic of consciousness. This text is important since it prepares the step to the realism of the laboring individual: indeed, to put it in the vocabulary of these early writings, alienation is not at all a matter of consciousness. Religious representations cannot be explained simply by consciousness.

In this sense now, an entirely new problematic arises when we read that religious man is man divided from himself. The first step into the concrete explanation of this division is to join the concepts of religious alienation to those of the state; this is done in *On the Jewish Question*,[50] also written in 1844. Marx tries to discover the roots of religious alienation on the level of the State.[51] This is a step into his proper direction—out of the schemes of consciousness, but only the first step. A year later, in *The German Ideology*, it is no longer the State that produces the split individual, but labor. Labor will appear as divided and dividing. The State was still another universal in which the individual estranges himself from himself.

The Ambiguity of Marx's 'Humanism'

1. The humanist concept of labor

The last section of the first manuscript of 1844 is entitled 'Estranged labor.' In it, as is well known, Marx develops the concepts of *Vergegenständlichung*, objectification; *Entwirklichung*, loss of realization; *Entfremdung*, estrangement or alienation; *Entäußerung*, exteriorization. The critique of labor, in this text, is 'humanist' since it considers the product of labor as taking away from man what is properly his own, so that "the worker loses realization to the point of starving to death." The theme is well known: Private property does what religion does, namely place man's genuine good out of his reach: "The worker is related to the product of his labor as to an *alien* object." "Whatever the product of his labor is, he is not. Therefore the greater this product, the less is he himself" (*MS*, 562/ *MEW* 40, 512/*MECW* 3, 272) etc....

Now, the concept of labor is assuredly humanist-universalist in these texts in the sense that through labor man loses his essence, his universal qualities. This remains thus the predominant scheme of thought in the text of 1844. But at the same time—and it is my purpose to develop, here again, the minor problematic in this text—another tone appears: "[T]he external character of labor for the worker appears in the fact that it is not his own, but someone else's, that it does not belong to him, that in it he belongs, not to himself, but to another" (*MS*, 565/*MEW* 40, 514/*MECW* 3, 274). In other words, another individual has taken away the object of his work as well as his work itself (*H* II, 14). The subterranean trend in Marx's humanism, as it is operative in his early analysis of labor, lies in the recognition that estrangement occurs between two individuals: one taking away from the other the product, his work, and actually part of himself. "An immediate consequence of the fact that man is estranged from the product of his labor [...] is the *estrangement of man* from *man*. [...] What applies to man's relation to his work [...] also holds for man's relation to the other man" (*MS*, 569/*MEW* 40, 517–518/*MECW* 3, 277). "[S]omeone else is the master of this object, someone who is alien, hostile, powerful, and independent of him. If his own activity is related to him as an unfree activity, then he is related to it as an activity performed under the yoke of another man" (*MS*, 570/*MEW* 40, 519/*MECW* 3, 278).[52] One could align many more quotations.

The picture that results from these texts should be clear: there is actually a double concept of man operative in Marx's concept of labor in these early texts. One concept of man is Feuerbachian and expressed in the vocabulary of the 'species being,' *Gattungswesen*: "In estranging from man nature and himself, estranged labor estranges the *species* from man." Here labor is seen as dividing man from his universal qualities: "Man is a species being [...] because he treats himself [in labor—R.S.] as a *universal*." He treats himself as a universal because in labor he appropriates what is necessary to sustain the species. "The universality of man appears in practice precisely in the universality which makes all nature [...] the instrument of his life activity" (*MS*, 566/*MEW* 40, 515–516/*MECW* 3, 275–276). The satisfaction of needs is seen, in this line, as the constitution and preservation of his universal essence, his human nature. "In creating a *world of objects* [...] man proves himself to be a conscious species being, a being that treats the species as its own essential being" (*MS*, 567/*MEW* 40, 516–517/*MECW* 3, 276). That occurs in labor everywhere, but labor is estranged when the species being becomes "alien to him," when it is turned "into a means to his *individual existence*" (*MS*, 567/*MEW* 40, 517/*MECW* 3, 277). In such labor he progressively gives away his bodily forces, his consciousness and finally his physical existence altogether simply to sustain his life. Thus, the universalist concept of man in this analysis of labor means: labor is always "man's active species life"; estranged labor, "in degrading spontaneous, free activity to a means, [...] makes man's species life a means to his physical existence" (*MS*, 568/*MEW* 40, 517/*MECW* 3, 277).

The second concept of man has nothing to do with this problematic of the universal. Here it is another man, another individual who alienates the laborer: "If the product of labor does not belong to the worker, if it confronts him as an alien power, then this can only be because it belongs to some *other man than the worker*. If the worker's activity is a torment to him, to another it must be *delight* and his life's joy. Not the gods, not nature, but only man himself can be this alien power over man" (*MS*, 570/*MEW* 40, 519/ *MECW* 3, 278). This text is decisive: first of all, it uses the language of conditions of possibility, second it traces the condition of possibility of alienated labor to the subject, third it announces the chief title with which Marx will, from 1845 on, characterize everything universal, all idealism: the gods *or* nature—the 'holy' (see *The Holy Family*, ironical for Bruno Bauer and his school of 'critical criticism'; "Saint Bruno," "Saint Max" in *The German Ideology*, for Bruno Bauer and Max Stirner).

The language of transcendentalism: This does not come through in Struik's translation. The German says: "*so ist dies nur dadurch möglich...*" (*MS*, 570/*MEW* 40, 519/*MECW* 3, 278). Marx's purpose is to explain how a worker can be disowned of the force, the enjoyment and the product of his labor. Answer here: such disownment is possible only on the level of individuals. There must be one individual to disown another individual (*H* II, 14). This is the second point. The individual replaces the species being in the explanation of alienated labor. What Marx calls reality is here no longer the accumulation of abstract human qualities, but the realm where one man appropriates what is necessary to sustain his life, and another disputes this appropriation to him. Thirdly, the polemic against "the gods" in this text, although a Feuerbachian theme when carried out in the schemes of the species being, becomes an indicator of Marx's newly discovered transcendentalism when it is juxtaposed to 'nature.' To speak of the 'nature' of man—that is now considered religious talk. "The gods on their own were never the lords of labor; no more was ‹ *nature* ›" (*MS*, 570/*MEW* 40, 518/*MECW* 3, 278).[53]

It is remarkable how this new language coexists in the first manuscript with the Feuerbachian language of *Gattungswesen*. Marx actually goes back and forth between the two intuitions that labor estranges the worker from his universal qualities of being human, and that he is so estranged by another individual. The coexistence is possible because of the *appearance* of logical clarity: the owner of the means of production is the *cause* of estrangement in granting the worker only "the smallest and utterly indispensable part of his product" (*MS*, 516/*MEW* 40, 475/*MECW* 3, 239), i.e., wages, and the species being is the *presupposition*, the presupposed reality, from which such capitalist robbery is possible; the presupposition that explains how capital is "stored-up labor" (*MS*, 526/*MEW* 40, 484/*MECW* 3, 247). But this sequence—the individual is the cause, the species being the presupposition of alienation—is only apparently coherent. Explaining estranged labor, first through the species being and then through the relation of individuals, joins heterogeneous elements: this is clear from the standpoint of the chief question that we are asking Marx: what is your understanding of reality? Once the question is raised in that fashion, reality cannot be both the species being and the individual.

Without knowing it and without willing it perhaps, Marx takes systematically the counter-position to Feuerbach, but in Feuerbach's language (*H* II, 15). For Feuerbach, under the title of 'species-being,' the genus is the totality of which the individual is only a particle. What one individual lacks, in Feuerbach's perspective, another has—and that is how mother nature fulfills her universals. In other words, that another profit from my labor is the very intention behind Feuerbach's notion of *Gattungswesen*. Just one text from Feuerbach on this complementarity at the heart of his notion of 'genus' (*H* II, 15): "Because Christianity ignores the 'genus,' which is the sole locus of solution (of conflicts), the sole locus of justification, redemption, and cure for the individuals' sins and defects, it needed some supranatural assistance towards the triumph over sin [...] But there exists a natural reconciliation. My fellowman is the mediator between myself and the genus [...] The sins and defects of particular human beings vanish in the genus which has no other appropriate existence than in the totality of mankind."[54] This text is clear enough about the resolution of the particular in the universal; the retribution of man's own activity estranged from him by private property.

In Marx's thinking, as it emerges in this first manuscript, what is real is not the genus. No such reconciliation in generic being takes place. Such subsumption appears to Marx, from 1844 on, explicitly as scandalous. There is not, there must not be, a universal reality beyond the individuals which distributes to them their predicates and reconciles abstractly their needs. No concept of 'Man,' then, who realizes himself in realizing this attribute or quality in an individual A and that attribute or quality in an individual B.

This same critique of universalism in the manuscripts of 1844 could be carried out with regard to money (*H* II, 16): it is money, indeed, which acts as the genus. Money is the genus as it was understood by Feuerbach: money is that power beyond the individuals which assigns them arbitrarily the predicates of being; it is that universal which possesses them; and the individual is only the locus where money realizes itself in always precarious forms of life. Marx's critique of "The Power of Money in Bourgeois Society" (section from the third manuscript) (*MS*, 631–636/*MEW* 40, 562–567/ *MECW* 3, 322–326)[55] aims at showing that such reconciliation in the universal 'Money' is illusory. The individual cannot be understood as a momentary actualization of such a universal; as the partial property of such a universal. In fact, in bourgeois society, that is what happens—and quite as Hegel before him, Feuerbach is the ideologist of that society. "Money's properties are my [...] properties and essential powers" (*MS*, 633/*MEW* 40, 564/*MECW* 3, 324).

2. The transcendental concept of labor

The ambiguity of Marx's notion of reality as it is operative in his critique of estranged labor in 1844 can be traced to a double meaning of man, in these texts. 'Man' designates, on the one hand, the *abstract* realization of the totality of attributes as it results from the complementary relations in civil society, and on the other hand the *concrete* realization of these attributes in *each* man (*H* II, 16). Only in the former case can 'labor' be understood in the Hegelian sense of negativity, i.e., as a process of objectivation (*H* I, 109/57).[56] Only in a realism of universals can one speak of "the labor of the negative." This does not designate yet the specifically human labor, but simply the activity of objectivation as such, the self-differentiation of the universal. 'Generic' labor here remains essentially linked to consciousness.

When Marx begins his economic studies in 1844, and at the same time discovers Feuerbach, he believes that the translation of the Hegelian concept of labor into a Feuerbachian 'anthropology' renders it concrete. Concrete labor is now understood by him to be reality or the 'real' objectivation—thus German metaphysics enters the domain of economy (*H* I, 110/58). This temporary fusion of economy and Feuerbachian anthropology explains the ambiguity of Marxian humanism in that year. But it is overcome the year that follows. In 1844 the properly transcendental concept of labor announces itself, but it is carried out for its own sake only in the writings that follow the epistemological break.

Another way to put the situation that we are faced with in 1844 is to say: labor is seen in two irreconcilable perspectives by Marx in these manuscripts: as generic labor and as individual labor (*H* I, 112/59). The inner structure of generic labor is objectivation: consciousness objectifies itself in the structure of opposition called labor. So, the content of generic labor is universalization: in the anthropological terms borrowed from Feuerbach, generic labor means opening oneself up to the universal, set one's spiritual energies free etc. Alienated labor, in this perspective, is the closure of labor; the reversal of the process of universalization; the necessity to work in order to eat, and not in order to free the resources of consciousness in him; the subordination of the generic activity to the vital requirements. The content of individual labor is not universalization. It is the satisfaction of basic individual needs. This concept of labor is opposed to generic labor as the individual is opposed to the species being; or again, as practice is opposed to theory (*H* II, 19). In anticipating what will have to be said about the notion of ideology in *The German Ideology*, we can add: the opposition between generic labor and individual labor is the same as between irreality and reality, or ideology and reality.

With regard to transcendentalism, there is a difficulty, now. Indeed, both the concept of generic labor and that of individual labor are transcendental, but not in the same way. Generic labor is only an offspring of the dialectic of the idea: i.e., the transcendentalism of a subsisting in-itself, the species being precisely. When we speak of a transcendental concept of labor in the early writings it is individual labor that is meant: the concrete realization of human attributes in one laboring individual.

In the light of this properly Marxian transcendentalism the concept of generic labor must again appear as "a fantastic realization of the human essence because the human essence does not possess a veritable reality" (*H* I, 120–121/64). This was said of religion, but applies to a transcendentalism of the in-itself of an idea in general. When the human essence does possess a veritable reality it is realized in a living individual and there is no need for such projection into universals.

The manuscripts of 1844 thus contain their own principle of destruction: the level on which moves the representation of universals as well as its critique is already sidestepped by Marx when he understands the realism of universals—religious, political, social, ideological universals—as a symptom of an essence "that is not realized on the level of reality." "Religious misery is, on the one hand, the expression of real misery and, on the other hand, protest against real misery." As opposed to 'real' misery, the miseries of religion, philosophy and the State are seen as symptoms of defects in what Marx calls here 'reality,' i.e., the reality of the laboring individual. "The critique of heaven thus transforms itself into the critique of the earth" (*MEW* 1, 378–379/*MECW* 3, 175–176).

A last remark on the ambiguity of Marx's 'humanism' in the texts of 1844 before we begin reading *The German Ideology*: that ambiguity can now be stated simply as a twofold understanding of man. On the one hand, 'man' means the neo-Hegelian 'generic being,' a universal, on the other hand it means the properly Marxian laboring individual. Now, this implies that we do not appropriately speak of man, in Marx's understanding, if we speak of him in terms of his nature, his species. Animals are understood once we know their species; but man cannot be understood that way. This is the only case in the history of modern philosophy that I can think of, in which, before *Being and Time*, we are told that we understand nothing of man if we compare his essence, nature or species to those of animals—or God, for that matter.

The Reversal of Problematics in 1845

We now have to see how the crisis in Marx's thinking reverses the order of what I called the minor and the major problematics in the early writings. I shall begin with some remarks on Althusser's concept of the 'epistemological break.'

1. The "epistemological break"[57]

The break of 1845, Althusser writes, divides Marx's thought into two main periods: the still 'ideological' period of the early writings and the 'scientific' period of all that follows after 1845. We are told that the total redefinition of concepts which this break entails is so radical that it puts an end to Western philosophy altogether. You remember that at the other extreme of Marxism, Marcuse had held the same position already in 1941.[58] I shall briefly sketch this concept of epistemological break through five points:

a) The 'break' sanctions the birth of a new science—in that sense it is 'epistemological.' Quite as with Galileo and with Freud, a new science appears in 1845, the Marxist science of history called historical materialism. Any science establishes its proper theoretical object. Not that the unconscious did not exist before Freud, or the earth not revolve around the sun before Galileo, and historical material conflicts not before Marx—they were not objects of theory. Althusser describes the break of 1845 as a pushing to the secondary realm of the categories of consciousness, and one can only agree. But what appears as the major problematic? The proper theoretical object constituted in 1845 is the concept of 'mode of production,' which includes as its main problems: concrete behavior in a society, organizational structures of such a society, the ideological discourse that a society holds of itself etc.... all notions related to the universal 'society,' to what Marx precisely denounces in 1845 as "the person, society." From this first remark on Althusser's concept of epistemological break—i.e., from the meaning of the word 'epistemological' in it—it should be clear that the break is not much of a break at all: it perpetuates, on the contrary, the problematic of universals which was that of the neo-Hegelians.

b) Now for the word 'break' in the concept of 'epistemological break.' It is said to separate two problematics: one ideological, the other scientific. The concept of 'problematic' in Althusser recovers approximately what other structuralists call a 'field,' that is, a domain of conceptual elements in a closed system ruled by unvariable laws. There is, according to Althusser, the 'field' of ideology prior to 1845, with its unvariable laws observable ever since Plato, and then there is the 'field' of scientific Marxism with its own unvariable laws. One could say that what is radical about the 'break' is that it constitutes ideology as ideology: indeed, before there was a problematic out of which ideology could be criticized, it did not exist as such, was not knowable as ideology. Here again, we can only agree that Marx takes a step out of the philosophy of consciousness and out of humanism—if for the time being that is what is to be meant by 'ideology.' So, what he steps out of is quite clear. What is not so clear is what he steps into; but what *is* clear again, is that there will be no way to hold at the same time that the step of 1845 leads Marx *both* into the realism of the laboring individual and into the problematic of scientific Marxism, since the latter rests entirely on universals—ultimately the Diamat!

c) The epistemological break, as seen by Althusser, is actually only inaugurated in 1845—it is continuous. That is understandable if we remember that the break is one between two 'fields,' two 'problematics.' Thus the ideological field will continue to coexist with the scientific field; even, Althusser says, the ideological field will indicate, at each period of Marxist science, which are the problems to be solved by that science. The way ideologists, at each moment of history, speculate about 'man,' indicates to scientific Marxism how man, at each time, has to be transformed into 'mode of production.' The new problematic appears at one moment, but then it has to re-articulate itself constantly in historical developments. In Althusser's terms, anti-humanism remains a constant task.

d) The epistemological break produces knowledge of society. Althusser speaks of the discovery of a new continent: whatever does not take root on that new continent "produces no knowledge." On this new continent *all* sciences come together. Marx has discovered the ground on which, from now on, knowledge can at all be obtained. The matter of such knowledge is 'society' or 'history.' Only after 1845 does one scientifically know what men do and what happens in history. Thus there is a pre-history of science, and then the firm establishment of that science. It is clear that such language rings more like Engels than Marx: and it is Engels who has perpetuated the realism of universals in laying the ground for the discovery of general rules or laws according to which social phenomena can be grasped theoretically. But it is this element of 'new laws' for knowledge which blatantly contradicts the realism of individuals that we have seen at work already in the texts of 1844 and which we shall see come fully to the fore in *The German Ideology*. Not a new method for science, but a displacement of the understanding of what reality is: precisely not graspable through universally valid rules and laws, but an always localized, finite, concrete effort to satisfy individual needs.

e) The epistemological break is theoretical. Althusser says, time and again, that the 'break' concerns science and ideology only in so far as they produce knowledge. It is this new knowledge that allows for interventions in history, that allows to act. The institutions of ideologies—religion, morals, legal convictions, political convictions etc.—are combatted only in so far as they claim to produce knowledge. The break only allows to 'judge' them—denouncing fictitious concepts of the bourgeoisie, such as "liberty and justice for all" etc., for the sake of scientific concepts derived from the knowledge produced by the working class, such as the "inexorable laws" of contradiction, overdetermination etc.[59]

These five remarks show with sufficient clarity, I believe, that the theoretical intention to identify 'structures' in society—superstructure and infrastructure—is only a new version of the realism of universals. This theoretical intention towards a Marxist science, once again, is as old as Engels, see some of Engels' titles (*H* I, 17/6): "Dialectics and Natural Sciences," "Mathematics and Natural Sciences" etc.[60] It is Engels who compares Marxism to Darwin, and who wants to show a compatibility with the positive results of other sciences at the time. Scientific Marxism deals with objective structures—economic and social on the one hand, political, legal, philosophical etc. on the other hand (*H* I, 406). Let me quote three lines from Engels in his article "Karl Marx" written for the *Popular Almanac*: "The ideas and beliefs [*Vorstellungen*] of each epoch are quite easily explained through the conditions of economic life of that epoch and by the social and political relations resulting from them."[61] This is 'Marxist science' reduced to its simplest expression. This is also the misunderstanding of Marx's own thinking in its simplest expression. Indeed, statements such as this—and how frequent they are in Marxist literature!—totally miss the reversal of the materialism of universals operated by Marx himself. 'Reality' does not mean for Marx, as Engels claims, 'matter,' which produces the spirit, but labor. Engels goes back directly to Feuerbachian intuitive materialism when he writes: "The idea that the material world, as it is perceived by the senses, constitutes the sole reality (is our discovery) [...] Our consciousness and our thinking, however transcendent they may appear to ourselves, are only the products of a material, corporeal organ, the brain. Matter is not the product of the spirit, but it is the spirit itself which is the highest product of matter."[62] ‹ Lenin writes: › "Marx has opened the path to the study [...] of social and economic groups [...] by revealing the origin of all ideas and all tendencies without exception in the state of the productive material forces."[63] This entire materialist 'science' retains intact the Feuerbachian horizon which is only a modified Hegelianism. Structuralist Marxism retains, not the materialist problematic, but the universalist problematic which, through Engels and Feuerbach, plunges its roots directly into Hegel. Witness: Althusser's interpretation of Mao's treatise "On Contradiction."[64]

2. The situation of Germany and the reversal of problematics

The turn towards reality, understood as finite and singular, arises quite clearly in Marx's critique of the "German anachronism" (*H* I, 128/65–66). "We have shared the restorations of modern peoples without having shared their revolution" (*MEW* 1, 379/*MECW* 3, 176).[65] It is due to an incapacity of life, a 'historical' incapacity, that "the sole domain where Germany is contemporary with history, on an equal footing with reality, is that of theory, of her philosophy" (*MEW* 1, 383/*MECW* 3, 180).[66] The theme is familiar: England's revolution is economic, France's is political, and Germany's is purely abstract, primarily a critique of religion. The passage from abstract to real, in what Marx calls simply 'Germany,' that is in the intellectual elite in Berlin and in Leipzig (see "The Leipzig Council," end of *The German Ideology*: that is where the left Hegelians were),[67] is a passage from religion to philosophy. Marx stigmatizes "the enormous cleavage between the claims of German thinking and the answers of German reality" (*MEW* 1, 386/*MECW* 3, 183). Here Marx steps actually out of philosophy of consciousness, out of the equation between consciousness and reality, denouncing that equation. A famous text on Luther denounces the illusion that interiorization means realization: "Luther has vanquished slavery by devotion, but in replacing it with slavery by conviction; he has broken faith in authority, but restored the authority of faith; he has dropped the chains of the body because he has burdened his heart with chains; etc." (*MEW* 1, 386/ *MECW* 3, 182). To such spiritual emancipation, Marx opposes the question: "Where is there, then, a *real* possibility of emancipation in Germany?" (*MEW* 1, 390/*MECW* 3, 186).[68]

Let us carefully look at the lines that follow in his *Critique of Hegel's Philosophy of Right*. "Here is our reply. A class must be formed which has radical chains [...]" (*CHR*, 182/*MEW* 1, 390/ *MECW* 3, 186). 'Must be formed,' this is 'our reply' (*H* I, 136/69): the class struggle here appears as an a priori construction in order to solve the German misery of being caught up in speculation. The social conditions for emancipation do not exist—hence a proposal. The proposal is Hegelian in inspiration: create one class that would contradict all others, "A class in civil society which is not a class of civil society, a class which is the dissolution of all classes." So, the translation of German, i.e., abstract emancipation, into concrete emancipation, this reality must be 'formed' in agreement with the 'German' presuppositions, i.e., with a philosophy of contradiction. But what is the goal? Precisely to step out of such philosophy of contradiction. To lead the German society from consolation through piety or speculation to real emancipation. Here the reversal in the problematics begins to be quite visible: Marx's goal is to use the problematic of universals for the sake of the concreteness of the individual. In the words of Shlomo Avineri (who can certainly not be accused of complicity with the theory of the realism of the laboring individual!—being one of the most Hegelian of Marxists): "For Marx there never is and never was, under any society, a preponderance of 'society' over 'individuals'; the phenomenon so described is the domination of some individuals by other individuals."[69] And this is what is meant in the text quoted: "What constitutes the proletariat is not naturally existing poverty, but poverty artificially produced" (*CHR*, 182/*MEW* 1, 390/*MECW* 3, 186–187). The situation of the proletariat is not a matter of 'nature' but of 'artifice.' And who are the agents of such artifice? The text says: "mass of people." And "mass of people" is opposed to "society" as a false entity: the proletariat "is not the mass of people mechanically oppressed by the weight of society, but the mass resulting from the disintegration of society." So, the proletariat is a construction meant to unmask the fiction of universals: "When the proletariat announces the dissolution of the existing social order, it only declares the secret of its own existence, for it constitutes the effective dissolution of this order" (*CHR*, 182–183/*MEW* 1, 391/*MECW* 3, 187). And to make the a priori construction of an artificial dialectic clear, Marx adds: "Just as philosophy finds its material weapons in the proletariat, so the proletariat finds its intellectual weapons in philosophy; and once the lightning of thought has penetrated deeply into this virgin soil of the people [that is: once the a priori construction of class dialectic has polarized the masses into two masses—R.S.], the *Germans* emancipate themselves and become *men* [*Menschen*]," i.e., 'real.' And for the shift towards 'reality': "Philosophy can only be realized by the abolition of the proletariat, and the proletariat can only by abolished by the realization of philosophy" (*CHR*, 183/*MEW* 1, 391/*MECW* 3, 187).

In the language of universals, of contradiction, and of dialectic we have here clearly the goal: emancipate 'men,' in the monadic plural, towards their 'reality.' The proletariat allows philosophy to realize itself through a concrete content. The mass which is to be constituted as the reality of the dissolution of society, gives philosophy its conditions of realization. Since the scheme of thought contradicts the content of thought, Marx still conceives of liberation as universalization; and yet, what kind of universal does he see at the end? The universalization of the negative, that is, universal disintegration; the dissolution into monads which already characterizes the proletariat. Thus the second indication for the reversal of problematics in 1845 has to be taken from Marx's concept of real emancipation.

3. The relation between Marx and Engels concerning their categories

A third indication can be gathered from the personal relation between Marx and Engels. I have already quoted some texts in which Engels speaks as the first to perpetuate the problematic of universals beyond Marx. On this entire matter a recommendable contribution is the article by Donald Hodges, "Engels' Contribution to Marxism."[70]

Marx and Engels meet for the first time in Cologne in 1842.[71] Marx is already known as the editor of the *Rhineland Gazette*, Engels is an unknown figure. The reception is cool. The friendship begins in Paris, at the end of 1843/early 1844.[72] Now, Engels belongs to a family of manufacturers, and Marx will call him the "cotton lord." He is at home in trade and industry. Avineri describes "the basic difference between Marx and Engels" in the following way: "Engels arrived at proletarian socialism through economic analysis and an historical study of the actual conditions of proletarian life in industrial centers. Much of the later different approach which always distinguished Marx from Engels can be traced back to this difference in background and intellectual heritage."[73] And Avineri is quite clear about Engels' philosophical competence: "Engels' ignorance of Hegel is sometimes unbelievable [...]"; his references to Hegel are "so badly distorted that one wonders what understanding Engels must have had of Hegel."[74] Avineri does not hesitate to say that *The Holy Family, The German Ideology, The Communist Manifesto*, although co-signed by Marx and Engels, "can be considered Marx's writings."[75]

Engels is Marx's first-hand information about the industrial situation in England: that is his main role. In 1842 Engels goes to Manchester; later he writes about this journey: "Here is what I felt with my fingers upon arriving at Manchester: the economic facts that have played no role, or only a despised role, in historiography, are, at least in the modern world, a decisive historical force; they constitute the basis from which arise the actual class oppositions [...] These class oppositions are in turn the basis of the formation of parties, of the struggle between parties, and hence of the entire political history" (written in 1885).[76]

When Marx begins to study—ferociously—political economy, the first notes that are left by him on these studies are summaries of Engels' articles on the situation in England, published in the *Franco-German Annals*.[77] The division of labor, so to speak, between the two is quite clear: Marx, in these years of the middle period, speaks as the philosopher, Engels as the economist. This happy conjunction worked out so well that they projected an impressive series of works which have never been written.[78] Engels says, again in 1885, that in 1845–1846 "Marx had worked out a materialist theory of history which was completed in its major features" when he met him in Brussels in August 1846.[79] And here is the type of questions Marx would put in writing to Engels who was in Manchester: "How often do you renew your machines? How do you handle the circulation of capital? How do you calculate the rotation of the circulating part of the capital, i.e., of the raw material, secondary material, and salary? How do you proceed in your banking operations? What categories of workers do you employ in your factory, and what are their proportions? Etc. etc."[80]

After Marx's death, Engels writes: all my life "I played the second violin, and [...] having a first violin as superb as Marx made me happy. Now I have to occupy Marx's place in the domain of theory and play the first violin. The blunders become inevitable, and no one knows it better than I."[81] The collaboration was closest in the political activities, particularly from 1848 to 1851. But we know that some letters by Marx to his wife, dealing with Engels, have been destroyed[82]—they seem to date from the period when Engels himself began projecting works on philosophy, namely the book *The Dialectic of Nature*, written from 1878 to 1883. The book remained incomplete and fragments were published only in 1925.

It is as a dialectician that Engels contradicts most blatantly Marx's own concepts. Engels' notion of dialectic is tied to 'matter' understood, as I have said, in the line of Feuerbachian naturalism—the

very title of Engels' book indicates this. Avineri calls this a "mecha-
nistic attitude" in dialectics, which reflects even in Engel's notion
of labor. Indeed, Engels views socialism as the scientific progress
of natural dialectics: 'things' have their own movement now, Avineri writes: "Engels' later remark about socialism as domination
over things and not over people fails to grasp the philosophical
significance of Marx's analysis of labour, since 'things' are objectified human labour."[83]

When Engels concludes his book *Ludwig Feuerbach and the
End of Classical German Philosophy* by saying that "the German
workers' movement is the heir of classical Germany philosophy,"
the bridge is complete that ties Marxism to neo-Hegelianism (*H* I,
149/78–79).[84] Engels adopts his materialism from the dialectics of
the generic being in Feuerbach—except that the generic being is
now called 'society' and its negation the proletariat or the working
class. The very dialectic which Marx had used in 1842 to advance
a first step into the non-dialectical reality of German society is now
taken up and simplified into a law of historical contradictions. Thus
Engels brings Marxism back into the mythology of a history developing by itself, as if history constituted a reality, an in-itself, unfold-
ing according to inherent laws (*H* I, 179/86). Such a view is that
of the early Marx, remaining under the sway of the 'generic being'
which alienates or objectifies itself and overcomes its alienation.
Such a reality would be infinite, and such a history would actu-
alize all its possibilities, all virtualities contained in its concept.
Once again, and to conclude on Engels: the line from Hegel through
Feuerbach and Engels to contemporary Marxism (Mao's "On Contradiction") bypasses the emerging problematic in Marx... although
Feuerbach is considered by Engels the last philosopher.

Since the key concept, as I have said at the beginning of the
semester, which divides Marx and the Marxists is that of practice,
and since the *Theses on Feuerbach*, written in Brussels in March
1845, deal explicitly with this concept, we shall have to elaborate
the realism of the laboring individual from this short text (*H* I,
314/138).

LECTURE 5

Practice as Motive Subjectivity
of the Concrete Individual

With the *Theses on Feuerbach*, we have the decisive answer to the
question 'what is reality?,' or 'what is being?' (*H* I, 356). Stated
negatively: reality is lost when one substitutes consciousness for
it. Stated positively: reality is heterogeneous when compared to
the categorial determinations of consciousness and theory. These
theses refute both the alleged creativity of thinking—which is the
cornerstone of dialectics—and what the ninth thesis calls "intuitive
materialism"... that of Feuerbach and later of Engels. What is now
dismissed is the entire problematic of a consciousness receiving
being, i.e., of intuitive consciousness—be it intellectual intuition
(Hegel) or sense intuition (Feuerbach) (*TF*, 67–68/*MEW* 3, 5–6/
MECW 5, 5).

1. Practice versus intuition

Now, what is that being which is no longer 'sense-given,' which
cannot be grasped by intuition? It is practice, and the practice of a
concrete human being apprehended in his particular situation. Only
when considered in his practice can one say, as the sixth thesis
does, "the essence of man is not an abstraction inherent in each particular individual." Feuerbach presupposes "an abstract, isolated,
human individual," since each individual realizes the "essence of
man" for him, as if each individual could be understood out of
such an essence. On the contrary, says Marx, man can be understood only as what he is in a situation determined historically and
socially. I already said that 'historical' and 'real' mean the same
thing for Marx, the same concreteness of a situated individual. This
is what is meant by the expression in thesis six: "In its reality [and
not, as the translation has it, in its 'real nature'!—R.S.], the individual is the ensemble of social conditions"—not the 'totality,' but

51

the ensemble as the concreteness of conditions in which it stands (*TF*, 68/*MEW* 3, 6/*MECW* 5, 4).[85]

Against the realism of universals, then, we read in the sixth thesis: "Feuerbach [...] is obliged [...] to conceive the essence of man in terms of a 'genus,' as an inner and mute universal quality which unites the many individuals in a natural way" (*TF*, 68/*MEW* 3, 6/ *MECW* 5, 4). 'Nature' and 'essence' are thus opposed as universals to "the many individuals."

We have always been told that the pertinence of the *Theses* against Feuerbach lies in the substitution of 'generic being' by 'social relations,' as just quoted. But what does 'social relations' mean here? That phrase remains unintelligible as long as it is not clarified by the reference to "the many individuals." And it is totally misunderstood if it is seen as presenting yet another hypostatization. It refers to nothing else but the living individuals entertaining among them relations for the sake of satisfying needs (*H* I, 318/140–141). They are not graspable through *theoria*, as they are for the dialectician, the Feuerbachian materialist, and also the structuralist. Any *theoria* seizes being as an object. It is this structure of being as 'objective' in the classical sense (confronting our faculties as a *Gegenstand*) which the theses on Feuerbach are intended to eliminate. Theory is now definitely transformed into practice—not as Feuerbach would have it, replacing intellectual or intelligible objectivity with sensible objectivity, nor as Althusser ‹ would have it ›, speaking of theoretical practice as a way of intervening in the play of contradictions, but "practical activity" as mentioned in the ninth thesis: "The highest point attained by intuitive materialism—i.e., the materialism that does not conceive sensibility as practical activity—is the intuition of particular individuals and of civil society" (*TF*, 68/*MEW* 3, 7/ *MECW* 5, 5). Thus, the pre-Marxian materialism 'considered' both the individual and civil society as Objects for intuition. The particular as well as the universal were objects for theory... the first, for sense intuition, the latter for intellectual intuition.

Marx opposes, as these lines state, "practical action," *praktische Tätigkeit*, to "*die Anschauung der einzelnen Individuen und der bürgerlichen Gesellschaft* [the intuition of particular individuals and of civil society]." This opposition is stated with all desirable clarity in the first thesis: "The chief defect of all previous materialism (including that of Feuerbach) is that the object (*der Gegenstand*), sensibility, are conceived only in the form of the *objects* (*Objekte*) *or of the intuition,* but not as *human sense activity,* not as *practical activity*" (*TF,* 67/*MEW* 3, 5/*MECW* 5, 3).[86] Marx's reversal affects primarily the status of theory, the 'seeing' of things in intuition (*H* I, 322/142–143). To be, for Marx, is to be active—not to be an object for intuition or science (Althusser). Considered in itself, action has nothing to do with the onlooking gaze that has been the attitude of philosophers in the West until Marx. Philosophy is thus finished in as much as it means *theorein,* manifestation of an object. Marx operates the ontological dissociation of intuition and action: they do not belong together. We can act without objectifying our action, that is, without giving it to ourselves as an object. And we can act that way precisely when basic needs and their satisfaction are at stake.

It is thus not enough to state that Marx substitutes practice for theory. The step from theory to practice is rather taken in two movements: Feuerbach had already substituted intuition for thought and theory; Marx, properly speaking, substitutes practice for *intuere,* 'input,' receptivity in any sense. Marx's reversal of transcendentalism is aimed directly neither at 'abstraction' nor at 'speculation,' as a superficial reading of the eleventh thesis against Feuerbach makes one guess ("The philosophers have only *interpreted* the world in different ways; the point is to *change* it" [*TF,* 69/*MEW* 3, 7/*MECW* 5, 5]). This thesis, in its all too short abridgement of Marx's discovery of reality, is to be read as a turning away from 'viewing,' 'interpreting,' 'seeing,' '*theorein,*' 'receiving'—all of which are as old as Platonic philosophy; and as a turning towards a totally different understanding of being. Being cannot be received by a beholder, it is what comes to be when man acts. The refutation of 'abstraction' and 'speculation' had, on the contrary, already been achieved with Feuerbach—with the limited success that we know, since Feuerbach's materialism was, in a sense, still more abstract than Hegelian spiritualism.

Being is acting, not looking. Action is possible, precisely, only insofar as it is not intuition—not the intuition of itself, or the intuition of some object (*H* I, 324/143–144). This ontological heterogeneity between intuiting and acting is Marx's philosophical discovery.

This heterogeneity can be described in the following way: when an object appears, i.e., when we intuit, action is paralyzed; and when we act, intuition is impossible. The point is that intuition demands a kind of distance, the 'step back' that the beholder has to take from the object intuited; whereas action is by definition immediately tied to what it acts upon. Thus the heterogeneity between intuiting and acting is the same as the heterogeneity between stepping back from things, and mingling among things.

This does not eliminate intuition or theory. But it localizes them. Once again, intuition and theory have their site of competence, their locus, which is assigned to them ontologically by the equation, in Marx, between action and being. There are then different domains of theory, which Marx works out in the later writings: political theory, economic theory, theory of ideologies, theory of history. But, as I have said, these regional theories remain misunderstood in their inner articulation as long as their ground is not seen clearly: the laboring individual. From there, it becomes understandable why in political theory, for instance, the concept of means of production has such a central place; or why 'geopolitics,' the analysis of geographical factors affecting power relationships, has to be a discipline within political theory.

2. The concept of subjective practice

The first thesis on Feuerbach begins with the following sentence: "The chief defect of all previous materialism is that things (*der Gegenstand*), reality, the sensible world, are conceived only in the form of *objects* (*Objekt*) *or of intuition*, but not as *human sense activity*, not as *practice*, not subjectively" (*TF*, 67/MEW 3, 5/MECW 5, 3).[87] In other words, in action, as it is understood by Marx, there is no place for seeing, intuiting; there is no object. That is what is meant when Marx says that practice is subjective.

We are far from the *Manuscripts* of 1844, in which man was objective in as much as he had outside of himself an objective world to which he relates; 'objectively,' there, meant the relation to objects. Now, the subjectivity that Marx opposes to such intuitive objectivity hits objectivity where it is theoretical: that is, the new concept of subjectivity is opposed to any relation between a subject and an object. Marx's concept of subjectivity is, in other words, deliberately anti-dialectic. The way in which he discovers reality excludes intentional otherness and the entire machinery of bridging otherness by noetic acts.

Useless to say that this is an entirely new concept of subjectivity (*H* I, 325/144–145). It is in this novelty of the concept of subjectivity that Western philosophy finds itself overthrown, displaced, reversed. At least what seems to have been most constant and most apparent in Western metaphysics is now overcome, namely the *theorein* with its sequel: either intellectual or sensible intuition. It is the very concept of being that undergoes a decisive mutation. Ever since Aristotle raised the question of being, it was raised in regard, in relation, in view (and these three expressions say a lot about the metaphysical character of even ordinary language) of the theoretician, i.e., man as the beholder. The theoretical attitude has remained the unchallenged horizon within which Western philosophy has proceeded. Subjectivity, within this horizon, was conceived as that which allows a thing to appear before the spirit; subjectivity was the objectivity of the object insofar as the object received its being from appearing before such a subject. This may still have been hidden in Plato and Aristotle—but the objective character of subjectivity comes totally to the fore in Descartes. And one can show that Cartesian dualism is laid out with the very discovery of objective laws in nature, in man, in community by Socrates. The subject–object dichotomy is not confined to the realm of modernity: modern philosophy only draws the explicit conclusions that were contained in the Greek notion of *theoria*. In other words, ever since Plato and Aristotle, the subject to which the world appears is the condition of possibility of objects. In Descartes, only, this subjectivity is clearly identified as thinking thing. But from Greece to Descartes to Kant, consciousness is transcendental because it gives to things their status of objectivity. The classical premise of metaphysics is that being resides in theory. It is with this presupposition of rationalism—that being is seen, known, knowable, rational—that Marx breaks in 1845.

So, what is meant in the first thesis on Feuerbach is by no means the transition from one concept of matter to another concept of matter—as if from a static notion Marx stepped to a more dynamic notion, now called practice or action. That would still be a mere transformation of dialectics, since a dynamic materialism, as it is developed so widely in Marxism, is understood to be dynamic only on the ground of ever new contradictions developing in 'matter.' No, the transition that the first thesis speaks of, is that from one notion of subjectivity to another notion of subjectivity. Marx steps from a receptive subjectivity—receptive of an object—to a subjectivity that is no longer receptive, i.e., from which any object relation is excluded. So, being is no longer anything that might offer itself to us for contemplation, nothing objective or sensible—in an entirely new sense, being is now 'subjective.' Entirely new, because this concept no longer has objectivity as its corollary. It is a subjectivity deprived of its objective pole.

Taken literally, this first sentence of the first thesis is simply not understandable, since it says two irreconcilable things at the same time. On the one hand, it says: The defect of past materialism was to conceive of objects as objects; on the other hand: we have to conceive of objects subjectively. What is meant, though, is quite clear: the entire problematic of *Gegenstand* disappears. What is meant is that reality, which hitherto has been viewed as object, no longer can neither be viewed nor an object. Reality is nothing *gegenständlich*, nothing objective. The true name of that reality, inasmuch as it is foreign to objectivity, is Marx's new notion of subjectivity. Stated otherwise: action is possible only as long as it is free of intuition, as long as it has neither object nor world in front of it (*H* I, 326/145).

In the old categories of ontology: Marx thus steps out of dualism. Since Descartes, ontology has been dualistic. Stepping out of dualism, however, Marx does not espouse a monism either—be it an immobile one as Parmenides', or a dynamic one as Hegel's. I said that on the problem of universals Marx has to be ranked among nominalists; now we see the reason of this: being as action is irreducibly manifold. Other thinkers after Marx, but both quite ignorant of him, think being in a similar fashion as irreducibly manifold: Nietzsche and Heidegger. Nietzsche never mentions Marx in his writings or notes; and Heidegger mentions him a few times, praising in an enigmatic statement his philosophy of history ("Letter on

Humanism").[88] But it is safe to say that neither Nietzsche nor Heidegger owe anything whatsoever in their understanding of being as manifold, to Marx.

Another remark can be made on this new concept of being in Marx by which being equals action. Namely, that it is what is best known by all. It is the reality that each living individual lives—and wholeheartedly so. The manifold, here, does not dissolve social constellations and the subject, as in Nietzsche; rather the manifold is the full recognition of subjectivity. To act in order to satisfy basic needs: no one can claim that he does not know what that means; and no one can claim that this is a universal in any way that would be more than purely verbal—or formal, if you want. The universal that a word is, 'action,' as a text says that I already quoted. The eleventh thesis against Feuerbach expresses this shift from theoretical dualism to polyvalent practice in the schemes of teleology: "The philosophers have only *interpreted* the world in different ways." It is the teleology of knowledge that is thus designated as the root of philosophy—not only Hegel's but philosophy ever since its beginnings. "The point is, to *change* it." In spite of the abridgement of the text—which seems to replace cognitive teleology with political teleology—the shift towards a new kind of telos is clear: telos of practice, of action. What this thesis does not say clearly is the polyvalence of action. But this becomes clear when we read it together with the first thesis, which was precisely about the individual.

Now, in a sense the interpretation of being as action, as production, dominates the entire thought of Hegel, already. To renounce action would be to renounce life; to renounce the struggle for recognition would be death for the individual. In that sense there is a priority of practice over theory that underlies much of Hegel—so that the eleventh thesis, short as it stands, somehow states what Hegel had already written before (*H* I, 332/147–148). Philosophy is the owl of Minerva that comes when the night falls—i.e., once the action is over. "Philosophy comes always late."[89] It is therefore hilarious to see Marxists take hold of the eleventh thesis against Feuerbach and claim that now philosophy has been, once and for all, buried and replaced with the science of action: political, economic, historical. "[W]hen philosophy appears, reality has already accomplished and finished its work of formation of the world."[90]

Thus for Hegel already, "the point is to change the world." But how does Hegel understand action? Work is understood by him as that which allows consciousness to become objective. Consciousness becomes objective in the mediation of an instrument that it uses, a tool. The instrument is the object of action, it is the action as object. And objectivity is at the end of action, too, for Hegel: to work is to realize a work, a piece of work. Hegel's notion of action moves entirely within the horizon of objectivity. Only thus can action after all not be mine: it is the action of the self-producing concept, the objectivation of the concept. But with this self-production of the mind, we are once again at the opposite pole from Marx: action is objectivation, hence production of something to be placed in front of our gaze. Practice thus becomes theory: contemplation of what has been rendered objective. In Hegel, everything is drawn to the side of theory, and thus unified; in Marx everything is drawn to the side of practice, and thus multiplied. Action, in Hegel, designates the process of objectivation for theory.

This theoretical concept of action was at work in the early manuscripts by Marx; it was their major problematic. Practice actualizing itself in labor was self-consciousness, recognition of the self in the other. Just one text from the first manuscript to show this: "The object of labor is therefore the *objectification of man's species life*: for he duplicates (*verdoppelt*) himself not only, as in consciousness, intellectually, but also actively, in reality, and therefore he contemplates himself in a world that he has created" (*MS*, 568/ *MEW* 40, 517/*MECW* 3, 277). Man duplicates himself in reality, and that is his action; he contemplates himself in what he has produced, and thus action is led back into theory. It is this subsumption of action under theory that disappears with the theses on Feuerbach. Hegelian action, or the action described by the lines from the first manuscript just quoted, then appears as pseudo-action, contemplation precisely.

Hegelian idealism and Feuerbachian materialism are thus overthrown in one movement when Marx steps from contemplation in action to action as satisfaction of individual needs. Action as idealist self-appropriation and materialism as intuitive appropriation are replaced with appropriation by the body. Marx does not dispose yet of a genuine vocabulary to express the transmutation of action. Therefore, in the first thesis on Feuerbach he borrows from Feuerbach the term 'sensible' to refer to such appropriation by the body: "The sensible world," he says, has been conceived erroneously in the form of objects; correctly conceived, the sensible world is "human sense activity, practical activity, action." 'Sense' and 'sensible' are meant here to suggest the concrete, always particular being of bodily action towards the satisfaction of needs.

One wonders how Marxists such as Althusser can so obstinately polemicize against the early writings when it is precisely the theoretical notion of action, put forward there, that they adopt. Labor is the self-production of a universal, in the Marxist tradition as well as in the *Manuscripts* and in Hegel: the self-production of a class. The title 'sensible' is introduced in the first thesis to negate any such representation of self-production of a universal (*H* I, 344). It is because sensible objects are particular that "real activity" is in turn particular, too... always other. "*Sinnlich menschliche Tätigkeit*," human sense activity, this is the first concept that introduces multiplicity into being—and brings philosophy back to Democritus and Heraclitus. We are far away from the Marxist talk about 'social practice' (*H* I, 348). Althusser's definition, very elaborate, of practice, which I have already quoted, shows again how practice, for the Marxist, is objective practice: "By *practice* in general I shall mean any process of *transformation* of a determinate given raw material into a determinate *product*, a transformation effected by a determinate human labor, using determinate means (of 'production')."[91]

Reality as the Production of Material Life

1. The 'German Ideology'

The German Ideology introduces an entirely new vocabulary: we
now have expressions such as 'the individuals that act,' 'the individuals that produce,' 'acting individuals,' 'living and acting individuals' (*H* I, 349)…[92] At the same time phrases are abandoned that
recall Hegel and Feuerbach, such as 'generic being,' 'mankind,'
'sensibility' etc.[93] Thus *The German Ideology* marks the end of idealist anthropology: the individuals replace 'man' at the same time as
action replaces 'intuition,' *Anschauung*.

Marxism has developed without knowledge of *The German Ideology*. This book was published for the first time in 1932, simultaneously in the *MEGA* edition and in the selection of early writings col-
lated by S. Landshut and J. P. Mayer.[94] The *MEGA* edition, and after
it the Dietz edition, have imposed a radical editorial regrouping of
sections on that text. It was impossible to reconstruct the originary
text out of the many leaflets; so, the editors have grouped them the-
matically, organized them more or less systematically, and at times
completed faulty passages. This order, particularly as it stands in
the first section of the book, on Feuerbach, has been challenged by
the discovery in the Amsterdam Institute for Social History of two
manuscript pages, until recently unknown. The *MEGA* conjectures
cannot be trusted therefore.

We know that writing huge manuscripts was for Marx a way of
clarifying his ideas for himself.[95] When he could not find a publisher
he abandoned his works without regret; this is what happened
to *The German Ideology*. In the preface to *The Critique of Political Economy* Marx writes that he and Engels had abandoned the
manuscript of *The German Ideology* "to the gnawing criticism of the
mice all the more willingly as we had achieved our main purpose:
self-clarification."[96] In another instance, that of *The Holy Family*, a
German friend of Marx's presented him, in 1867, with a copy of that
book written in 1844. Marx wrote to Engels: "Kugelmann possesses

a much better collection of our works than both of us put together. Here I also found *The Holy Family* again; he has presented it to me and I will send you a copy. I was pleasantly surprised to find that we do not need to be ashamed of this work, although the cult of Feuerbach produces a very humorous effect upon me now."[97]

Useless to say that Engels, after Marx's death, dismissed *The German Ideology* very curtly: "Before sending these lines to the press, I have once again ferreted out and looked up the old manuscript of 1845/46. The finished portion consists of an exposition of the materialistic conception of history which proves only how incomplete our knowledge of economic history still was at that time."[98] Of course, since in 1888, when Engels wrote these lines, 'materialism' for him had come to mean the dialectics of nature, a movement immanent to material conditions of production—and not, as in *The German Ideology*, the concreteness of the laboring individual. One understands that Engels, in 1888, would never co-sign passages such as this: "The materialistic view of the world [...] is *not without premises*, but it empirically observes the actual (*wirklichen*) material premises, and for that reason it is, for the first time, an *actually* (*wirklich*) critical view of the world" (*DI*, 274/*MEW* 3, 217/*MECW* 5, 236). And what is '*wirklich*'? "With the theoretical equipment inherited from Hegel it is, of course, not possible even to understand the empirical, material attitude of [these] people" (*DI*, 274/ *MEW* 3, 217/*MECW* 5, 236). Hence "one has to leave philosophy aside" insofar as it is "theoretical garment." Marx then says that this path towards 'reality,' *Wirklichkeit*, was already indicated in his earlier publications, "but since at that time it was done in philosophical phraseology, the traditionally occurring philosophical expressions such as 'human essence' (*menschliches Wesen*), 'species,' etc." were misleading (*DI*, 274/*MEW* 3, 217–218/*MECW* 5, 236). These lines quite clearly describe the 'break' in Marx's thinking—which obviously Engels never understood. Wherever that was possible, the German editors have distinguished between Engels' contribution to the manuscript and Marx's.[99] It appears quite clearly that Engels wrote transitions and titles—editing work. For instance the title of the first part, chapter one, is from Engels: "Opposition of the Materialist and Idealist Outlooks." The Soviet publishers go still further in Engels' editing (with an eye on dialectics), in introducing all the titles placed in parentheses in the table of contents. They indicate a common tendency towards a philosophy of contradiction and resolution of contradiction.

2. Marx's empiricism versus 'German Ideology'

The expression 'German Ideology'—I have said that—is actually a tautology in Marx's usage. For instance, against the Socialists in Germany he would polemicize, saying that "they do not see, in the Communist literature from England and France, the expression and the product of a real movement; they rather view this literature as purely theoretical, as having emerged entirely out of the 'pure thought,' quite as they figure the German philosophical systems have. [...] The German ideology, in which these 'true Socialists' are caught does not allow them to see the real conditions" (*DI*, 481/ *MEW* 3, 441/*MECW* 5, 455). Thus, 'German ideology' is the old habit of German philosophy to consider reality as sprung from the concept—whereas in France and England, communism, although it may have taken on systematic forms at times, has sprung from 'reality.'

So, to the German ideological equation between the concept and reality, Marx opposes the phrase "empirical reality" (*H* I, 351). The word 'empirical' has now taken the place that, in the *Theses on Feuerbach*, was that of 'sensible.' Sense reality, in the *Theses*, was the still insufficient title for Marx's discovery of being as activity. Empirical reality, now, is the appropriate title for that discovery. What constitutes empirical reality in *The German Ideology* are the empirically traceable acts of an individual by which it satisfies its needs, "men living empirically," actions "verifiable empirically," "empirical conditions created by real men in their real relations." "[P]hilosophers have not depicted social relations as the mutual relations of particular individuals identical with themselves, and the laws of nature as the mutual connections of these particular bodies" (*DI*, 538/*MEW* 3, 427/*MECW* 5, 442). To the 'German ideology' is thus opposed the relation between monadic individuals; and what kind of relations? Those of their bodies—that is, satisfaction of bodily needs. The German ideology is of the type of the "valiant fellow" that Marx speaks of in the Preface: "Once upon a time a valiant fellow had the idea that men were drowned in water only because they were possessed with the idea of gravity. [...] That valiant fellow was the type of the new revolutionary philosophers in Germany" (*DI*, 9–10/*MEW* 3, 13–14/*MECW* 5, 24).

What is essential in this critique of German ideology is to see how empiricism, as Marx has now come to understand it, opposes at the same time and identically philosophy of consciousness and dialectics. The book begins with the well-known lines: "Hitherto men have always formed wrong ideas about themselves, about what they are and what they ought to be. [...] Let us liberate them from the chimeras, the ideas, dogmas, imaginary beings under the yoke of which they are pining away. Let us revolt against this rule of concepts" (*DI*, 9/*MEW* 3, 13/*MECW* 5, 23). And, on the rejection of dialectics: "[T]he abolition of a state of affairs in which relations become independent of individuals, in which individuality is subservient (*Unterwerfung*) to chance, and the personal relations of individuals are subordinated (*Subsumption*) to general class relations, etc. [...] [is what we are concerned with—R.S.]. We are therefore here concerned with individuals at a definite historical stage of development and by no means merely with individuals chosen at random. [...] The individuals' consciousness of their mutual relations will, of course, likewise be completely changed [...]" (*DI*, 534/*MEW* 3, 424–425/*MECW* 5, 438–439). Relations become independent of individuals when they have their own logic, i.e., when they are considered as dialectical in themselves; then individuals are '*unterworfen*' and 'subsumed' under general class relations. Marx explicitly criticizes the '*Verselbstständigung*' of individual relations into class relations. And it is because of such a rejection of class dialectics that consciousness is seen as derivative of the recognition of the empirical realism of the laboring individual.

But this notion of empiricism that Marx opposes to the German ideology is again very personal and must not be confused with what is traditionally called empiricism (*H* I, 352). Marx says in this text that "the premises are men—not isolated and fixed in some imaginary way, but taken in their process of real development, in determinate conditions, a development that is visible empirically.

As soon as one represents this process of life activity, history ceases to be a collection of lifeless facts as it is with the empiricists [...]."[100]

Empiricism, indeed, is traditionally opposed to rationalism: experience, rather than reason, is the source of knowledge. But when Marx criticizes empiricism, to exalt at the same time empirical reality, it is a theory of knowledge that he criticizes: the British empiricists, he argues, are interested in producing an account of how ideas are built up in the knowing individual: refuting that they are innate and claiming that they are derived from sensation and reflection upon sensation. But Marx's problematic is not at all that of the certainty of our knowledge. What he polemicizes against is empiricism as a theory of knowledge—as such, empiricism does not speak of what Marx calls "the premises from which we begin" (*DI*, 16/*MEW* 3, 20/*MECW* 5, 31). 'We,' i.e., versus idealists and empiricists alike.

Let us look at the brief but decisive section entitled (by the editors) "Premises of the Materialist Conception of History" (*DI*, 16–17/ *MEW* 3, 20–21/*MECW* 5, 31).[101] "The premises from which we begin are not arbitrary ones, not dogmas, but real premises from which abstraction can only be made in the imagination." At the outset we have thus the opposition between 'reality' and 'imagination.' This line gives us a further clue to the title 'German ideology'; on the side of ideology, we have the arbitrary, dogmas, abstraction through imagination. This does not mean, however, that we possess as yet a satisfactory notion of ideology. This concept is simply opposed here to 'reality.' On the side of reality, then, we have the following description: "[The premises from which we begin—R.S.] are the real individuals, their activity and the material conditions of their life, both those which they find already existing and those produced by their activity. These premises can thus be verified in a purely empirical way." On the side of 'reality,' opposed to the German ideology, we have: real individuals, actions, material life conditions, all that which can be established empirically ('*auf rein empirischem Wege konstatierbar*'—not 'verifiable,' as the translators put it: that would again be the language of a theory of knowledge).

Neither idealism nor empiricism can deliver us from dogmas and arbitrary abstractions, but only a radical thinking that is not theoretical; that does not 'consider,' be it ideas or 'lifeless facts' (*H* I, 352). The old example of the runner can be helpful here: as an object of intuition, as a fact, as a sensible, objective datum, his running is there for everyone to be seen. What the spectators view is the appearance of running—they themselves remain in their seats. This is how Feuerbach understood materialism: what can be sensed. And this is also how the empiricists understood what is empirical: what can be investigated and verified. But the reality of running is located not in the beholder, not the *theoria*, but in the act of running, in the subjectivity of the runner, in the lived experience. And this is precisely given only to the individual that runs. Now, we are not all and always on the cinder track; but we are all and always engaged in the activity of living. Thus there is a radical opposition in action itself as these lines oppose it to the German ideology. Action itself can be either *viewed*, i.e., abstractly imagined from the seats of the stadium, or "capable of being established *empirically*," i.e., experienced in the very acting. Empirical, real, concrete refer to the immediate, un-mediated, experience that the individual has of action itself. This was clearly stated in the first thesis on Feuerbach, namely that practice is subjective—not viewable as objective. Theory does nothing, literally. Theory necessarily leaves the being of activity outside, it withdraws from the effectivity of doing.

Such is precisely the status of what I called regional theories:

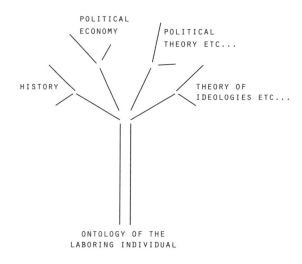

The regional theories are 'theories,' i.e., they step back from the phenomenon so as to view it according to laws; as theories, they re-introduce into Marxian thinking what the critique of the German ideology had thrown out: contradiction, wholes that are determined by contradiction, hence dialectics and resolution of conflicts. On the level of regional theories, terms such as 'empirical,' 'subjective–objective,' 'theory and practice' recover their traditional meaning. The best-known section in the book *The German Ideology* is precisely such a regional theory: historiography as based on the division of labor (part IV). Marx there traces contradiction to previous forms of labor: the basic distinction being that between material and mental labor. From this contradiction arise more derivative contradictions, such as between town and country, commerce and industry etc. But to oppose such types of activity, to say that the distinction between material and mental labor underlies all other forms, is to abstract from one's own laboring subjectivity—to objectify it, saying: at this very moment I am laboring intellectually. But such a sigh is different from the activity as such.

The realism of universals which was the major problematic in the early writings survives as minor problematic in the later writings in the regional theories—that is to say, basically in a strategic context. What I call here the ontology of the laboring individual, which is not dialectical, is what Marx calls "the first premise of all human history."

"The first premise of all human history is, of course, the existence of living human individuals." And note the passage quoted in the footnote: "The first *historical* [underlined—R.S.] act of these individuals, distinguishing them from animals, is not that they think, but that they begin to *produce* their means of subsistence" (*DI*, 16/ *MEW* 3, 20/*MECW* 5, 31). Capital text! It is placed in a footnote only because it is repeated later in the text.[102] Man is no longer thought of as '*animal rationale*,' but as '*animal laborans*'—as producing his livelihood. The 'rational' side of man comes in only in a derivative form: "Ideology itself is only one side of this history" (*DI*, 16/ *MEW* 3, 18 n./*MECW* 5, 29 n.). That is, consciousness, abstraction, reasoning, are ontologically derivative, secondary. It is secondary with regard to the immanent reality of action. The spectator, the one who does not act—and, in material historiography, or historical materialism, the non-worker—transforms activity into a spectacle; he transforms, by his gaze, practice into theory. This had already been strikingly stated at the end of the first manuscript of 1844: "The worker's *real, practical comportment* (*Verhalten*) in production [...] appears in the non-worker confronting him as a *theoretical* attitude (*MS* 575/*MEW* 40, 522/*MECW* 3, 282).

You see how this pivotal notion of practice puts into question the action which would be thinking, theorizing (*H* I, 354). That is precisely not an action that is immediate. Thinking understood as action objectifies: it is, for instance in the intellectual, related to the production of livelihood only mediately. Theoretical practice, to use Althusser's phrase, is not genuine practice since, quite as Feuerbachian sense-activity, it possesses another structure than life-sustaining immediate practice. Theoretical practice is altogether a practice of objectivation. As such it is not 'real,' 'empirical,' or, as the lines just quoted also say, 'historical.' Marx vigorously rejects, first in the *Theses* against Feuerbach and then throughout *The German Ideology*, any such identification between theory and practice: the German ideology consists precisely in replacing practice with theory: i.e., outside of 'Germany.' "We must look at the whole spectacle from a standpoint beyond the frontiers of Germany" (*DI*, 13/*MEW* 3, 18/*MECW* 5, 28). 'Germany' now stands for ideology pure and simple.

How does one so step outside of 'Germany'? By considering the body. That is a necessary consequence of the rejection of theoretical activity. The text on the premises of the materialist conception of history continues: "the first fact to be established is the physical organization of these individuals" (*DI*, 16/*MEW* 3, 20–21/*MECW* 5, 31). The physical activity of individuals is reality; the mental activity is idealism, ideology, theory. In the physical activity there is no otherness, no 'viewing,' no dialectic involved.

This distinction between physical activity and mental activity further helps us to clarify Marx's vocabulary and the status of the regional theories. Indeed, the word 'history,' quite as earlier 'the empirical' and 'the objective' appears twice: once on the ontological level, and once on the level of the regional theory called historiography. 'Historical' means, on the one hand, concrete bodily activity—always located in time and space as it is, always the doing (or running) of one particular human being. On the other hand, 'historical' means the tracing of developments through time: developments of the modes of physical activity by which people have satisfied their basic needs. Marx continues: "We cannot here go either into the actual physical nature of man, or into the natural conditions in which man finds himself—geological, oro-hydrographical, climatic and so on" (*DI*, 16/*MEW* 3, 21/*MECW* 5, 31). And Marx adds that these conditions "determine the entire further development, or lack of development, of men up to the present time."[103] Thus the concrete 'historical' bodily activity determines the 'historical' development of man which is traced in the regional theory called historiography. Therefore other regional theories will have to deal with geology, oro-hydrology, climatology etc. "All historical writing [historiography—R.S.] must set out from these natural bases [...]" (*DI*, 17/*MEW* 3, 21/*MECW* 5, 31).

Marx sums up the ontology of the laboring individual: "By producing their means of subsistence, men are indirectly producing their material life itself" (*DI*, 17/*MEW* 3, 21/*MECW* 5, 31). The very title 'historical materialism' is ambiguous, since it designates on the one hand the regional theory that traces the modes in which men have produced, at different moments in time, their material lives. But on the other hand, if we retain the ontological significance of 'historical,' 'historical materialism' is the very title of the ontology of the laboring individual: historical then means 'concretely located' (on the cinder track), and materialism, that reality is 'bodily,' the production of the means of subsistence. The regional theory of historical materialism is operative in the historical writings such as *The Class Struggles in France* etc. But always underlying is the historical materialism understood ontologically.

The Representational Status of Regional Theories

1. The ontological and the theoretical concepts of practice

The chief 'premise of the materialist conception of history' was formulated in *The German Ideology* (*H* I, 356): "The way in which men produce their means of subsistence [...]. This mode of production must not be considered simply as being the reproduction of the physical existence of the individuals; rather it is a definite form of activity of these individuals [...]" (*DI*, 17/*MEW* 3, 21/*MECW* 5, 31). The chief premise is the activity by which an individual produces its life; that is Marx's notion of practice. But quite as 'subjectivity,' 'materialism,' 'history' earlier, here too, Marx's concept is over-determined. Indeed, practice so described is what I called the ontological notion of practice. At the same time, *The German Ideology* contains a theoretical notion of practice, belonging into the regional theories.

The ontological notion of practice is stated clearly, in the same text, with reference to being: "As individuals express (*äußern*) their lives, so they are." 'Express' is a poor translation. '*Äußern*,' exteriorize, designates—not an outward manifestation of what is within a man—but life as not-interior; the merely exterior making of a living. That this practice is to be called ontological appears again from the next sentence: "What they are coincides with their production [...]." The individuals' being is their production of their own lives. These lines are, of course, capital for Marx's understanding of reality. Even one should not speak of 'practice' but only of 'practices,' actions. Practice is always located in a laboring individual: "What individuals are depends on the material conditions of their production." These vary. And so does their practice. Since practice is the bodily activity, it cannot be the same, ever, in two individuals. Each individual is localized by his body. So, when Marx says that the ontological notion of practice concerns the "physical reproduction of existence," "the way in which men produce their means of subsistence (*Lebensmittel*)," he speaks of the principle of individuation: practice as production of means of subsistence 'makes' the individual. In the term *'Lebensmittel,'* as an indication to the ontological concept of practice, we must not see, of course, an indication of mediation, *Vermittlung.* Practice at this level is immediate (*DI*, 17/*MEW* 3, 21/*MECW* 5, 31).

The theoretical concept of practice, on the contrary, is one of mediation. Here we have the Marxist notions of 'social practice,' 'revolutionary practice,' 'theoretical practice.' They all are located on the level of the political. Thus they all pertain to a problematic of the universal—the state, or classes. The universal cannot be a matter of practice in the first, ontological sense, since that basic type of practice is circumscribed, confined, situated by the limits of our body. The universal has its locus elsewhere than in the limits of the body: it has its locus in theory. Social or revolutionary practice is theoretical practice: it requires a political theory, that is, an objectivation of modes of exchange as they obtain at a given moment and in a given universal (in a given society). The first thesis against Feuerbach concluded: "He does not grasp the significance of 'revolutionary,' 'practical-critical' activity": one could not be clearer about the activity meant here. 'Practical-critical' shows that the revolutionary activity is a theoretical one.

These remarks take nothing away from the articulateness, the necessity, the intellectual rigor of revolutionary activity as theoretical. They only want to show the roots of such activity. At the root of social or revolutionary activity there is no *theorein*, no vision of totality; no intuition but only need. The theoretical concept of practice, on the contrary, requires that I take into consideration the whole, the totality of a given social reality; that I step back from it in the theoretical distance so as to seize it according to its laws. Literally, social or revolutionary practice requires a vision of totality; such a vision is theory. Theory is thus grounded upon the movement of seeing, upon the transcendence that renders seeing possible—transcendence as stepping outside, or beyond, a given object for contemplation. Ontological practice does nothing of the like. Ontological practice does not rise above itself.

We now can see more clearly the status of what I called regional theories: they literally re-present ontological practice. Ontological practice is 'rendered present again' in theoretical practice. Theory is a 'taking up again' of what happens in life when it sustains itself individually. This taking-up-again is the essence of the theoretical. A theory renders present to thought what exists outside of thought, the way in which "individuals exteriorize their lives." The status of theoretical practice—and of regional theories in general—will be understood fully only if we succeed in holding together, in seizing the intimate link, between representation and universalization. To represent an individual activity is to lose its individual character. Representation can never be of something individual. And representation can never be practical. Representation, universalization, and theory go together.

It is this distinction between ontological and theoretical practice that the eleventh thesis against Feuerbach conflates into one: "The philosophers have only interpreted the world, the point is to change it." The practice that changes the world is revolutionary, social practice—but *that* is precisely not what puts an end to the philosophers' interpretation of the world! On the contrary, that is the new form of interpretation, of theory, of universalization, of representation. The 'practice' that puts an end, once and for all, to the philosophers' interpretation of the world is the ontological practice of satisfaction of physical needs.

2. The theoretical origin of the division of labor

The same duplicity in the notion of practice appears in *The German Ideology*. Indeed, the section printed immediately after the one entitled (by the editors) "Premises of the Materialist Conception of History," deals with "Production and Intercourse. Division of Labor and Forms of Property—Tribal, Ancient, Feudal." In other words, we now steer into history in the sense of a theory of universals; we now proceed in the realm of representation. We represent such universals as "feudal society" etc., and we have the classical genealogy of property: from tribal property to communal and state property to feudal or estate property (*DI*, 18–19/*MEW* 3, 21–22/*MECW* 5, 32–33). It is clear that Marx here reasons on a totally different level than when he says that "what individuals are coincides with their production."[104] It is this difference of level that I suggest by the concept of representation.

It is not the task of this course to trace Marx's historiography; but it is a task, at this point, to show why the transition to the theory called historiography requires the intervention of the key concept of division of labor. With the step towards theory—or rather theories—arise such wholes as 'movement of society,' 'the march of history,' 'social practice' etc. Now, how do hypostases such as these 'move'? By conflicts that divide them; by contradictions that oppose parts of them; by dialectics, in other words. The march of giants such as 'society,' 'classes' etc. is possible as self-opposition only. Society opposes itself and thus proceeds through history. Ontological practice certainly does not move these giants—for the good reason that the essence of ontological practice does not reside in the general.

In the early texts the division of labor appeared as a fact: a fact that is bad for man, that alienates him (*H* I, 253ff./109ff.). And we saw how the concept of division of labor, in those texts, was only an application of Hegelian labor as objectification to the Feuerbachian species-being. What does the division of labor do theoretically? It explains the existence of classes and their struggle. The status of the concept of division of labor is genealogical. A theory is sought for that could explain the conflicts in society; a theory that explains the production of classes. The division of labor—that is the division of that whole called 'labor,' *die Arbeit*—proposes itself as the ultimate locus from which such explanation is possible.[105] The division of labor is the foundation of social classes, past, present and eventually future. This link between the genealogy of wholes in society and division of labor appears clearly in our text: "How far the productive forces of a nation are developed is shown most manifestly by the degree to which the division of labor has been carried" (*DI*, 17/*MEW* 3, 21–22/*MECW* 5, 32). And: "Each new productive force [...] causes a further development of the division of labor" (*DI*, 17/*MEW* 3, 22/*MECW* 5, 32).

This representational and genealogical status of the division of labor—i.e., its essential link with regional theories—appears blatantly in the way it is tied to property: "The various stages of development in the division of labor are just so many different forms of property [...]" (*DI*, 18/*MEW* 3, 22/*MECW* 5, 32). The first form of the division of labor is called '*naturwüchsig*'—a difficult term in *The German Ideology*, but designating that which is not produced by man; so the translators are correct to put: "the natural division of labor existing in the family" (*DI*, 18/*MEW* 3, 22/*MECW* 5, 33). Here it is physical strength and the like that determines the division of labor among members of the family. But "the division of labor becomes really a division only from the moment when a division appears between manual and intellectual labor," i.e., when it is taken out of the realm of the 'natural.' It is this primary division between manual and intellectual work that produces the chief social division, the third, in our text, between town and country. Intellectuals live in cities. When a new form of division of labor appears in the manufacturing halls, a new type of society arises: thus the division of labor is the genealogical origin of social formations.[106] But the division of labor allows precisely to speak of social formations, which ontological practice does not. Hence the origin of the division of labor is theoretical; it is theoretical practice that traces wholes and contradictions among individual practices. The origin of the division of labor is in representation.

The German Ideology shows this transition from the laboring individual to the division of labor quite clearly. "The fact is, therefore, that definite [*bestimmte*; better: determinate—R.S.] individuals who are active productively in a determinate manner, enter into these determinate social and political relations." The transition is clear: social relations are derived from, secondary with regard to practice as individual. "Empirical observation must in each separate instance bring out empirically, and without any mystification and speculation, the connection of the social and political structure with production." Social relations 'render present again,' in other words, they represent, practice as individual. "The social structure and the state are continually evolving out of the life process of definite individuals [...] as they *actually* or really are, i.e., as they act, produce materially [...]" (*DI*, 21–22/*MEW* 3, 25/*MECW* 5, 35).

Representation is the transformation of personal force into objective force, social force. On the level of personal activity, force, practice, there is no division—how could the individual activity, as activity, be divided, unless we take it in the Hegelian mode, as an activity of consciousness? Division of labor appears only once social formations confront the individual; once the individual sees himself in conflict with social entities. But to see himself so, he has to step out of the business of sustaining his life; he has to transcend, objectify, represent that business. The division of labor is thus one of the "echoes of the life process" (*DI*, 23/*MEW* 3, 26/*MECW* 5, 36). Since the object of 'theory' is, by definition, a universal, and since a universal 'moves' by inner contradictions, an element of contradiction is found in any theory: this element of contradiction is called 'division' and 'struggle.' Furthermore, the contradiction is one of forms universalized from practice—hence 'classes'—and practice when universalized is called labor. Thus the division of labor and the struggle of classes are meta-theoretical elements that are found in all theories as theories. I call 'meta-theory' the inquiry into those elements that are common to all regional theories.

One quote from *The Poverty of Philosophy* suggests this meta-theoretical character of the division of labor: "The very moment civilization begins, production begins to be founded on the antagonism of orders, estates, classes, and finally on the antagonism of accumulated labor and actual labor. No antagonism, no progress. This is the law that civilization has followed up to our days. Till now the productive forces have been developed by virtue of this system of class antagonism" (*EP*, 693/*MEW* 4, 91–92/*MECW* 6, 132). In other words, the history of civilization; the economy of the accumulation of labor; the political science of estates, classes etc.—all theories, in so far as they deal with human history, must be understood out of the 'law' of division of labor and class struggle. We are far from the formulations dealing with the transcendental condition of possibility of history: "Since we are dealing with the Germans, who are devoid of premises, we must begin by stating the first premise of all human existence, and, therefore, of all history, the premise, namely that men must be in a position [...] [of] eating and drinking, housing, clothing and various other things" (*DI*, 28–29/*MEW* 3, 28/*MECW* 5, 41–42).

And please notice the twofold usage of the concept of history here again. Marx continues: "The first historical act is thus the production of the means to satisfy these needs, the production of material life itself." But then this historical deed of satisfying our *Notdurft* is said to be "that one historical deed, a fundamental condition of all history"—history now taken in the sense of periods and ages. Now Marx describes how history in the theoretical sense emerges from history in the ontological sense: "[T]he satisfaction of the first need, the action of satisfying and the instrument of satisfaction which have been acquired, leads to new needs; and this creation of new needs is the first historical act" (*DI*, 29/*MEW* 3, 28/*MECW* 5, 42). And now for the division of labor, which belongs to this second, theoretical concept of history: this paragraph ends with the following remark: "further development [occurs] through increased productivity, the increase of needs, and, what is fundamental to both of these, the increase of population. With these there develops the division of labor [...]" (*DI*, 32/*MEW* 3, 31/*MECW* 5, 44).

The theoretical origin of the concept of division of labor is further made clear by the reference to Adam Smith. In *The Poverty of Philosophy* we are told: "Just as Adam Smith discovered the *division of labor*, so Mr. Proudhon claims to have discovered '*constituted value*'" (*EP*, 675/*MEW* 4, 77/*MECW* 6, 120). Marx's notion of division of labor does not remain economic, it penetrates into all other regional theories—but it retains from Adam Smith precisely its theoretical, not ontological, status. On the ontological level there is no division, since "division of labor only becomes truly such from the moment when a division of material and mental labor appears" (*DI*, 33/*MEW* 3, 31/*MECW* 5, 44–45). In a still other vocabulary Marx says that in the division of labor the individual is subjected to the slavery of the accidental (*H* I, 256): "[T]he abolition of a state of affairs in which relations become independent of individuals, in which individuality is subject to what is accidental, and the personal relations of individuals are subordinated to general class relations—the abolition of this state of affairs is determined in the final analysis by the abolition of division of labor" (*DI*, 534/*MEW* 3, 424/*MECW* 5, 438).[107] To understand the derivative character—derived from elementary practice, hence theoretical—of the division of labor it is enough to understand that "division of labor and private property are, after all, identical expressions" (*DI*, 35/*MEW* 3, 32/*MECW* 5, 46). In elementary practice, there is no division, no property, no class: "the classes [are—R.S.] already implied by the division of labor: they separate out in every such mass of men" (*DI*, 35–36/*MEW* 3, 33/*MECW* 5, 46). On the level of primary activity there is only a 'mass,' *ein Menschenhaufen*.

But what is the chief notion by which Marx describes the transition from the 'substantial' practice to the 'accidental,' i.e., class practice? It is that of pre-capitalist society.

3. The meta-theoretical concept of history

At first sight, Marx's notion of history, as operative in the regional theories, is totally linear, understandable, teleological.

I only have to remind you of some famous lines from the *The Communist Manifesto* about the class struggle and the division of labor:[108] "The history of all hitherto existing society is the history of class struggles. Freeman and slave, patrician and plebeian, lord and serf, guildmaster and journeyman, in a word oppressor and oppressed, stood in constant opposition to one another, carried on an uninterrupted, now hidden, now open fight etc. [...]" (beginning, after Preface).[109] Here history appears as driven by the class struggle. An actor dies on the battlefield of the classes, but that struggle soon rouses new actors. And then: "Our epoch, the epoch of the bourgeoisie, possesses however this distinctive feature: it has simplified the class antagonism."[110] So, with the interdependence of planetary industry the historical process becomes simplified. History itself engenders this simplification. This movement "is going on before our own eyes. Modern bourgeois society with its relation of production, of property and of exchange, [...] is like the sorcerer who is no longer able to control the powers of the nether world whom he has called up by his spells,"[111] etc.—Such is the one side of Marx's concept of history as theoretical, the history that historiography deals with.

But there is another concept of history, not evolutionary or revolutionary, but quite different. In fact, it contradicts the first. It appears in the *Grundrisse* in the treatment of pre-capitalist society. There history is not seen at all in a line of continuous development, moved by the invention of means of production and distribution of property, with the class struggle that ensues. There is a radical discontinuity between pre-capitalist society and capitalist society. I try to trace this other concept of history in order to clarify the meta-theoretical element that would lie at the heart of what I called earlier representation.

Pre-capitalist society is seen here out of the perspective of capitalist society. As such, it appears as the realm of free work, of the tie to the earth (called the "natural laboratory"),[112] of the communal exchange. It is characterized by the absence of private property and hence of division of labor, but at the same time by its belonging to the land, the soil. We are to think, I suppose, of the nomad's attachment to the land. What counts is that the individual here belongs at the same time to the land and to the community. These three terms can only be understood one out of the others.

Just as a reminder: Marx distinguishes between three such modes of production: Asian despotic, that of Antiquity, and the Germanic feudal. In each of these three cases the tribal community determines the mode of production. What counts, now, is that in each of these cases, too, the basic community is preserved by the despotic, or imperial, or feudal state. There is no separation, as there is today, between the Asian community and the despotic state; between the Mediterranean community and the Roman empire; between the Germanic community and feudal states. In antiquity men were inseparable from the land—and it is in one and the same movement that they become owners of private property and citizens. Thus the modern state differs radically from the Roman empire. Only today is there the possibility for man to lose his private property, since he lives under two determinations.

This contradicts flatly the broad statements of the *Manifesto*. Particularly the perennial character of the communal form contradicts the dramatic developments throughout history: pre-capitalist society is not moved by the class struggle. The class struggle only appears with the industrial revolution. Before that crisis, history, as understood by Marx in this line, was rather repetitive; cyclical; bent backwards; always returning to the soil; aiming at a restoration of the communal form (see the 'return' of the past in *The Eighteenth Brumaire*).

Now, this notion of repetitive (vs evolutionary) history seems to me quite useful as a meta-theoretical concept. Indeed, in its ties to the earth, the soil, and to the community it appears as a quasi-extension of the body. If the separation of the individual and the community is as impossible as the separation of the individual and the land, then the threefold unity is of a very physical kind. And further: the industrial revolution, then, tears man himself apart in tearing him away from this bodily unity; this unity into which he is 'incorporated.' The enigma of history, or the rise of dialectical history, is then the dissolution of that unity. The opposition of classes is an event, datable. It is the event in which man stands out of the community, sees the others as opposing him, and the event of the arrival of capitalism. The dialectics of change begin with the opposition between labor and capital. Here we have universals; but on the meta-theoretical level of the bodily incorporation of man into the community and the land there is no such dialectics, no division of labor in the strict sense yet. With that event, division enters into man's body: the division separates man from himself. There is no longer a communal body, in capitalism, Marx says, but only the phantom.

4. From representation to ideology[113]

We retain: the regional theories derive from the ontology of the laboring individual through representation. In political economy, historiography, etc., individual practice is 'rendered present again' but as obeying laws which are universal and which primarily have the character of contradiction. Now, this is the Marxian concept of representation in Marx; but there is another concept of representation in *The German Ideology* which leads us directly into the problem of ideology. Here is one of these texts, from the polemic against Max Stirner: Saint Max "is critical only of those ideas that are the 'mere offspring of his brain,' i.e., general concepts about existing conditions reproduced by the brain. Thus, for example, he does not even resolve the *category* 'Fatherland,' but only his personal opinion about this category, after which the *general valid category* still remains [...]. He wants to make us believe that he has destroyed the category itself because he has destroyed his emotional personal relation to it—exactly as he wanted to make us believe that he has destroyed the power of the Emperor by giving up his fantastic conception of the Emperor" (*DI*, 136/*MEW* 3, 109/*MECW* 5, 126).

Fantastic conception, emotional personal relation to categories, general concepts about existing conditions reproduced by the brain: this designates the ideological concept of representation. This entire text, with regard to the categories, seems to sweep categories all together into the basket of ideology. And the ideological concept of representation cannot be stated more succinctly: Saint Max "takes the world as his conception [*Vorstellung*—the translators should have put 'representation'!—R.S.] of the world" (*DI*, 136/*MEW* 3, 110/*MECW* 5, 126-127). But then, in this same text, the properly theoretical concept of representation emerges, too: Saint Max, we are told, "has still not *touched* these ideas [such as 'Fatherland,' Emperor, etc.—R.S.], insofar as they express *actual* relations (*wirkliche Verhältnisse*)" (*DI*, 137/*MEW* 3, 110-111/*MECW* 5, 127). Here we have the theoretical concept of representation—the concept of representation that founds theories.

From this twofold notion of representation—as fantastic conception and/as expressing actual relations—we shall be able to better understand the complex phenomenon that Marx designates as 'Ideology.'

The Categorial and the Creedal Concepts of Ideology

Against Stirner: "The man who, as a youth, stuffed his head with all kinds of nonsense about existing powers and relations such as the Emperor, the Fatherland, the State, etc. [...] this man, *according to Saint Max, actually destroys all these powers* by getting out of his head his false opinions about them [...]. But he does not even react critically towards ideas which are valid for others and are current as categories; he is critical only of those ideas that are the 'mere offspring of his brain,' i.e., general concepts about existing conditions reproduced by the brain. Thus, for example, he does not even resolve the *category* 'Fatherland,' but only his personal opinion of this category, after which the generally valid category still remains" (*DI*, 136–137/*MEW* 3, 109/*MECW* 5, 126).[114]

1. Theoretical categories versus 'fantasies' of belief

From this text, and others, it appears clearly that we have to distinguish between two kinds of representation: theoretical representations and ideological representations in the narrow sense. Theoretical representations operate with categories: these are said to remain 'generally valid' even after the ideological 'delirious fantasy' has been destroyed. The critique against Stirner, here, consists in accusing him of neglecting theory, and thus perpetrating under the guise of theory ideological representations which he only claims to have done away with. Stirner continues, indeed, to define man by consciousness... i.e., by belief.

Ontological practice is represented theoretically by the categories; it is represented ideologically by belief. 'Representation' is thus the largest concept that encompasses both theory and ideology.

However, and I have said that, representation itself is at times called 'ideology' by Marx. So that we have a categorial concept of ideology, and a creedal concept of ideology. All theories are ideological in so far as they are "echoes of the life process" (*DI*, 23/*MEW* 3,

26/*MECW* 5, 36) although they represent the 'real' life process, or they represent the life process 'concretely.' But ideologies in the strict sense represent the life process abstractly, in belief, i.e., in autonomous universals. Ideology in the strict sense designates the entire domain of representations *in so far as they become autonomous*, i.e., in so far as they constitute an in-itself—such as, precisely, 'Fatherland, Emperor, State.' One could say that ideological concepts are theoretical categories hypostatized.

The cultural sphere is altogether the object of theory. But in so far as it exhibits a semblance of autonomy, this sphere is ideological in the strict, creedal, sense. One believes in such abstract universals as freedom, imperial power—as long as one does not establish quite concretely what the imperial power of Ferdinand I of Habsburg really was, who would abdicate in the wake of the upheavals in 1848 and be replaced by Francis Joseph (–1916!); who would have to battle against the rising nationalisms, after the Congress of Vienna, in Italy, the Slavic countries, Germany; who would have to confront the powers of France, Russia, and England, etc.... Such a concrete tracing of imperial power is theoretical. But 'personal opinions,' 'emotional relations' are the reflection of abstract universals such as 'freedom as such,' 'imperial power,' 'state as such,' etc.... Of these, Marx says that Hegel impoverished them to the status of empty categories, i.e., ideological concepts: this reference to Hegel is clear in the section entitled 'Peculiarity,' still against Stirner: for Stirner, "the historical data are only names for a few simple categories [...] all worldly relations are only disguises, different designations, for the meagre content which has been assembled in the *Phenomenology* and *Logic*" (*DI*, 357/*MEW* 3, 282–283/*MECW* 5, 301).[115] Implicit in this quote is, as often, the praise for the concrete—categorial—starting point in Hegel, and the criticism of the total impoverishment of these concrete categories, into meagre universals. A quote from a letter by Marx to Mehring shows this creedal status of ideology more precisely: "Ideology is a process achieved by a so-called thinker consciously, it is true, but with a false consciousness. He is not aware of the real driving motives—only for this reason it is an ideological process" (*MEW* 39, 97/*MECW* 50, 164).[116] Ideology does not take into account the real driving motives—the need for elementary satisfaction—whereas theory does.

'A thinker,' then, is one who essentially abstracts. And in that sense we 'think' whenever we rave about 'human freedom,' 'Society,' 'Public virtue,' 'values,' etc. "Saint Max transforms a definite historical act of self-liberation into the abstract category of 'freedom'" (*DI*, 358/*MEW* 3, 283/*MECW* 5, 302). The status of abstraction, in *The German Ideology*, is opposed to that of categories: properly speaking, then, we would have to say that by categories we 'represent,' and by ideology we 'abstract.' This has nothing to do, of course, with 'abstract labor' in *Capital*.

Thus with the narrow sense of ideology—uprooted ideas about morality, religion, metaphysics, Marx says—the universals surface again, but, of course, as what Marx deliberately rejects. The criterion for distinguishing between theory and ideology is autonomy: whether thoughts are considered as expressions of life itself or, on the contrary, treated as if they were independent from the life activity, Marx sometimes speaks of ideology as referring to universals in so far as they lose their autonomous character and enter into theory: "Morality, religion, metaphysics, and all the rest of ideology, as well as the forms of consciousness corresponding to these, no longer retain the semblance of independence. They have no history, no development [i.e., as strictly ideological—R.S.]. But men, developing their material production and their material intercourse, alter, along with their actual world, also their thinking and the products of their thinking [i.e., theory—R.S.]" (*DI*, 23/*MEW* 3, 26–27/*MECW* 5, 36–37).

Against the abstract, universal products of thought, i.e., of belief, Marx retains what he calls the concrete name, that is, the category as concrete representation: in Stirner's developments on right, he observes, Stirner "smuggles in, in *advance*, the more concrete name, in this case 'Sultan's right,' in order to be able more confidently *later* to bring in his universal category of 'alien right'" (*DI*, 377/*MEW* 3, 298/*MECW* 5, 316–317). Philosophers of consciousness thus universalize the categories; they hypostatize the 'names' that theories deal with into an entity that is considered beyond history. An ideology is always deprived of the moorage that ontological practice provides—it is the effort to deprive categories of such moorage. Consciousness is ideological in as much as it declares: such moorage does not count, does not exist.—One might observe that the very elucidation of originary practice is 'thinking,' not 'knowing,' and that Marx's polemic zest plays a similar trick on him when he confines thinking to ideologies as when he declared all history, in the *Manifesto*, to be the history of class struggle.

Concepts such as 'right,' 'freedom'—to use only the ones from the quote above—have therefore a double status: concrete and theoretical on the one hand, abstract and ideological on the other. In a theory (political, historical, economic) I trace Right and Freedom with regard to concrete given relations to practice: as such they are then categories: right and freedom of the medieval serf, of landowners, of the industrial worker, etc. You see that the wholes we deal with in the regional theories are concrete wholes, whereas in ideology the same concepts are applied to free-floating wholes such as right in itself, freedom in itself, man as man, woman as woman, etc.... When categories become ideological—when they cease to be categories—they drift away and one can say anything whatsoever about X 'as' X.

Theory asks: what freedom, what 'Fatherland,' in what respect? Whose power, and over whom, in what conditions? If questions are raised in that way, we step from ideology to theory; from belief to categories; from abstract universals to concrete wholes.

Marx thus denounces the pretension that thought has to modify reality by modifying the representation that it makes of reality (*H* II, 24). The categories, since they 'echo' the life practice, remain in contact with reality—they can become strategic, they can modify realities such as political unity, classes etc., realities that are, in turn, derived from the primary practice of satisfying needs. But ideology will never be able to produce such modification.

2. The proportionality
"reality : representation :: reality : irreality"

It is clear, now, that this proportionality is more complicated than it may appear (*H* I, 368/160). At first sight representation = ideology = irreality. But there are texts in *The German Ideology* in which Marx declares that the opposition between reality and representation is trivial. The proportionality has therefore to be refined;

reality : representation :: theory : ideology. To call the universals that regional theories deal with 'representation' is to exclude any transcendence. Universals are not real, they are representations: that is to say, subjectivity is the essence of reality. No transcendence à la Hegel or Feuerbach can break this immediacy, this indistinguishability in what an agent does to satisfy his needs. Reality—or being—is found in its total incapacity to step beyond itself, that is, beyond need, hunger, suffering, work. This radical immanence of reality is what Marx calls 'life.' Representation in universals is nothing real: it only produces the categorial determinations of that reality. See this text: "This conception of history thus relies on expounding the real process of production—starting from the material production of life itself—[...] describing it in its action as the state, and also explaining how all the different theoretical products and forms of consciousness [...] arise from it [...]" (*DI*, 46/*MEW* 3, 37-38/*MECW* 5, 53). The negation of transcendence then means that between reality—or 'life'—and its representation there is at the same time continuity and discontinuity: continuity in so far as the categories in theory are really derived from practice, and discontinuity in so far as they are only categories, unreal. In this sense, the proportionality enunciated in the title is correct. But we have seen that 'representation' means two things: theoretical categories and ideological belief.

Ideology in the strict sense, then, is the ensemble of those representations which consciousness forms *spontaneously*—as opposed to derivatively. Marx's ontology is one that denies all spontaneity to thinking—or that localizes, rather, spontaneity in the realm of fiction. Such spontaneous thought creations are: images, memories, ideas, notions, schemes, reasonings, and—more sophisticated—all -isms: idealism (of course), but also humanism, republicanism, and communism, if that title is to stand for more than a strategic theory. The Germans "detach the communist systems, critical and polemical writings from the real movement of which they are but the expression" (*DI*, 551/*MEW* 3, 442/*MECW* 5, 456). From here it is evident that one has to question Althusser's opposition between ideology and science—as if, with the epistemological break in 1845, Marx had discovered a new "continent of science." This does not work for the simple reason that both science and ideology are representation, whereas the discovery that Marx claims is on the contrary that of the distinction between representation and reality. One unreal element (science) cannot define another unreal element (ideology) unless one first produces a notion of what reality is. In *The German Ideology* it is in vain that one would look for the alleged opposition between science and ideology.

Marx calls the properly ideological representation (as opposed to the theoretical one) "canonization of the world": "the transformation of real collisions, i.e., collisions between individuals and their actual conditions of life, into ideal collisions, i.e., into collisions between these individuals and the ideas which they form or get into their heads" (*DI*, 339/*MEW* 3, 268/*MECW* 5, 287). An ideal collision is any contradiction between 'I' and 'Society,' for instance. A real collision is between 'I' and 'my boss who robs me of the surplus value.' Of these real collisions we have theories; of the ideal collisions we have ideologies. In this same text, Marx also calls the real contradiction—which appears only on the level of theory—the '*Urbild*,' prototype, and the ideal contradiction the '*Abbild*,' ideal copy. This is exactly the reversal by which transcendence is abolished: in classical idealism, the *Urbild* is ideal, and the *Abbild* practical, real. Stirner, against whom all this is directed, thus remains an Idealist "who manages to transform the real collision, the prototype of its ideal copy, into the consequence of this ideological pretense [*ideologischer Schein*—see Kant—R.S.]" (*DI*, 339/*MEW* 3, 268/ *MECW* 5, 287).

An ideology can be defined in several ways: by its remoteness, through abstraction, from originary practice; by the universalist character that it gives to its concept; and by its elimination of the essence of reality, i.e., the subject: "The real relations are the relations of the individuals themselves, and declaring them to be relations of the non-ego only proves that one knows nothing about them" (*DI*, 331/*MEW* 3, 262/*MECW* 5, 281). Transcendence and ideology move within relations between entities separated from the individual: that is the third way of defining ideology. Abstraction, universalization, separation from the individual—all point to the same proportionality mentioned earlier.

Marx thus moves against his early position, and explicitly so: to hypostatize "the relation of the non-ego to the ego" is to fall into

"the wholly abstract phrase of alienation" (*DI*, 332/*MEW* 3, 262/
MECW 5, 281). Alienation now occurs twice: as theoretical category,
and as ideological abstraction. In the first line of analysis the task is
"to describe actual individuals in their actual alienation and in the
empirical relations of this alienation"; in the second line, "the set-
ting forth is replaced by the mere idea of alienation, of 'the' alien, of
'the' holy." In this text, as already earlier, the illusion is described as
an exercise in separating the category from its basis: thus Marx can
accuse the idealists of "the substitution of the *category* of alienation"
for real alienation... "to retain this philosophical expression for the
time being" (*DI*, 332/ *MEW* 3, 262–263/*MECW* 5, 281–282). The
mechanism of ideology is stated quite clearly in this text: it consists
in "accepting in good faith the [...] speculative expression of reality,
divorced from its empirical basis, for reality" (*DI*, 333/*MEW* 3, 263/
MECW 5, 282).

Marx goes very far in the denunciation of such abstract entities:
"the common name used, such as state, religion, morality, etc.,
should not mislead us, for these names are only abstractions from
the actual attitude of separate individuals" (*DI*, 337/*MEW* 3, 266/
MECW 5, 284). You are familiar with this critique of the state, which
leads to the theory of its withering away. Already in *On the Jewish
Question* he wrote: "In the state, where man counts merely as one
of his kind, he is an imaginary link in an imagined chain of sover-
eignty, robbed of his individual life and endowed with an unreal
generality." The terminology is clear: reduction of man to one of
the species, imaginary link between individuals, robbery of individual life, unreal generality: these are just as many traits that are
common to any ideology. I say he goes very far, since what is 'real'
about the state and all other abstractions is the way these abstract
wholes are 'lived' by the individual: "these objects, in consequence
of the totally different attitude towards them of the unique individuals, become for each of the latter *unique* objects, hence totally different objects, which have only their name in common" (*DI*, 337/
MEW 3, 266/*MECW* 5, 284–285). This is one of the texts in which
Marx's nominalism appears most clearly.

The two notions of representation or of ideology then can be summarized: as a category, a representation or ideological concept is
operative; the development of such operative (strategic) categories

is a theory. But as "a mere name" a representation or ideological concept is inoperative; *"renouncing the idea of* [*this*] *collision,"* (*DI*, 340/*MEW* 3, 268/*MECW* 5, 287) of state, of emperor, etc. operates nothing, is *unwirklich*, unreal.

LECTURE 9

The Heterogeneity between Being and Consciousness

From the critique of ideology we can—and must—draw some consequences with regard to the question raised at the beginning of the course: *ti to on*; What is being? When one quality, one category "assumes an abstract, isolated character, if it confronts me as an alien power [...] this by no means depends on consciousness"; and then Marx brings in an illuminating series of oppositions which begins with the opposition *Bewußtsein–Sein*: "It depends not on *consciousness*, but on *being*; not on thought, but on life; it depends on the individual's empirical development and manifestation of life [...]" (*DI*, 310/*MEW* 3, 245/*MECW* 5, 262).

There appears an ontological heterogeneity (*H* I, 377/161–162): representation turns out to be heterogeneous with regard to its pretense to be real. Representation has ontological claims which it cannot hold. The ontological inequality between consciousness and being is the thesis that underlies the entire *German Ideology*. In the traditional vocabulary, Marx explains this opposition sometimes as that between true and false consciousness: "Philosophers have declared people to be inhuman [i.e., "that the real man is not man"—R.S.], not because they did not correspond to the concept of man, but because their concept of man did not correspond to the true concept of man, or because they had no true understanding [*nicht das wahre Bewußtsein vom Menschen*—R.S.] of man" (*DI*, 523/*MEW* 3, 415–416/*MECW* 5, 430). "They detach the consciousness of certain historically conditioned spheres of life from these spheres and [...] transform the relations of these particular individuals into relations of 'Man'" (*DI*, 551/*MEW* 3, 442/*MECW* 5, 456).

What is excluded by texts like these is the very possibility to attribute to consciousness, to knowledge on the whole, any radical ontological significance. What has ontological significance is not the act of knowing and its transcendental structures, but the act of living and its transcendental structures. Why? Because of the indistinguishability of actor and acted-upon in the act of living. This indistinguishability is by definition excluded from conscious-

ness, since consciousness, or knowledge, is always consciousness
of, knowledge 'of.'

1. "In Ideology men appear upside-down"

This is the ontological significance of the entire critique of '*theorein*,'
contemplation, objectification: philosophy of consciousness posits
being in front of the knower. But such positing, such 'presentation'
of being as an object is lost with the recognition of the immediacy
of life and being in the practice of satisfying needs. You remember
the famous axiom: "*Das Bewußtsein kann nie etwas anderes sein
als das bewußte Sein*," "Consciousness can never be anything else
than conscious being, and the being of men is their actual life-
process" (*DI*, 23/*MEW* 3, 26/*MECW* 5, 36; *H* I, 378/162–163). The
point is that consciousness, i.e., "ideas, opinions and conceptions,"
as it is understood by Marx, has nothing to do with what is origi-
narily lived, with the real essence of life. Consciousness is what
representation ascends to: "In direct contrast to German philosophy
[i.e., all philosophy as philosophy of consciousness—R.S.] which
descends from heaven to earth, here it is a matter of ascending from
earth to heaven" (*DI*, 23/*MEW* 3, 26/*MECW* 5, 36). Phrases such as
this, repeated over and over in Marxism, are correctly understood
only in the context that has been guiding this entire course: the
question of reality, of Marx's understanding of being.

The ontological heterogeneity between being and consciousness is indeed stated in terms of a reversal; these formulations are
known: 'putting Hegel back on his feet' is in every text book, and
here: "If in all ideology men and their relation appear upside-down
as in a *camera obscura*, this phenomenon arises just as much from
their historical life-process as the inversion of objects on the retina
does from their physical life-process" (*DI*, 23/*MEW* 3, 26/*MECW*
5, 36). This is by no means the simplistic reversal of reverse Hegelianism that we are usually served! The effect of *camera obscura*
is historical: the "historical life-process" cannot dispense with this
reversal; the realm of ideology, in the large as well as in the narrow
sense, is an inescapable product of that life process. Here Althusser
has stated very correctly that ideology is something we have to live

with always—quite as for Kant, the mind cannot but produce transcendental illusions.

The effect of inversion—*camera obscura*—affects representation as well as belief: "what men say, conceive, imagine," i.e., theory as well as "morality, religion, metaphysics and all the rest of ideology." All products of consciousness, theory as well as fantasy, fall under this verdict of inversion. But what is the inversion? Precisely to set out from them rather than to lead up to them; to take representations as the '*primum notum*,' instead of originary practice. The denunciation of the inverse procedure followed by the Hegelians, when properly understood, indicates the entire program of reformulating ontology as I have tried to do it. The technical term, here, is once again borrowed from Hegel: 'determination.' But it receives another sense: "It is not consciousness that determines life, but life that determines consciousness" (*DI*, 23/*MEW* 3, 27/*MECW* 5, 37). In Marx's usage, here, determination means representation, not individuation.—Contrast this with Marxism: "The universal only exists in the particular, a principle which Mao reflects [...] in the following universal form: contradiction is always specific and specificity universally appertains to its essence. [...] [This pertains—R.S.] to the condition of a scientifically specified universality. If the universal has to be this specificity, we have no right to invoke a universal which is not the universal of this specificity." So, the only thing that changes from Hegelianism to Marxism, is the modality of the universal: no longer that which is operative in "the abstractions or the temptations of 'philosophy' (ideology)," but scientific universal, theoretical universal.[117] What is real, to Mao and Althusser, remains, then, the universal as specified in a historical situation—only a variation on Hegel.

But consciousness as it is understood by Marx has nothing to do with the originary lived experience (*H* I, 378/162–163); the universal of consciousness has nothing to do with reality; specification or individuation have nothing to do with determination. Furthermore: this signification of the concept of consciousness is found throughout Marx's writings; it never varies after 1845. 'Consciousness' always means 'being conscious of,' representing, judging, taking notice of, becoming aware of. In the *Grundrisse*: "If the worker 'discovers' that the products of his work are his, if he 'condemns' the

93

dissociation of his conditions of realizing them, and if he 'judges' that an intolerable situation is imposed upon him, he will have acquired an immense 'consciousness.'"[118] Discovering, condemning, judging, consciousness—all these are terms that pertain to representation. In *Capital*, too, consciousness is never reality itself, but it stands for, represents the economic process. Consciousness is situated with regard to originary practice: the bourgeois representation of that practice is 'situated' differently than the proletarian. *As* representation, consciousness lets go of reality.

Language, too, thus depends essentially on life, on practice and its site which alone is originary. Existence of language is due to need. No identification, here, between language and being (as in a certain breed of Structuralism). All characteristic traits of language and consciousness must be understood in the light of that one fundamental character: they are carried, supported by the life-process, secondary. Here again, vs Althusser: "The real [...] can only be defined by its knowledge; [it] is identical to the means of knowing it, the real is its known or to-be-known structure, it is the very object of Marxist theory."[119] Between Marx and Marxism the opposition concerning what is real is as clear-cut as between originary practice and its representation in theory. But it is ideology that claims: the real is the rational, the theoretical, the represented. For Marx, truth no longer resides in the spirit, but in doing. And untruth alone lies in the spirit, in so far as from doing it derives concepts that are not theoretical but fictions, ideological.

The entire polemic against Stirner shows that in his praise of the individual, the individual is still understood as consciousness; that for individual life, Stirner has substituted individual consciousness. Furthermore, this polemic also shows that such substitution is not simply an omission on the part of the philosophers, but that it occurs always in life; that life itself operates like a camera: reversing the relations of representation and making us believe that what we do is the consequence of our representations (*H* I, 394)! Thus private property believes in 'right,' law, and concludes that from the owner's ideas about law his property belongs to him. But his ideas on this matter simply arise from the way in which he satisfies his basic needs: by robbing someone else of his labor force.

And this consequence for the status of the categories: they operate dialectically, but only as categories! "For M. Proudhon, who sees things upside down, if he sees them at all, the division of labour [...] precedes the workshop, which is a condition of its existence" (*EP*, 773/*MEW* 4, 153/*MECW* 6, 186). And in the same text, Marx calls theory the 'organ' of reality: "They no longer need to seek science in their minds; they have only to take note of what is happening before their eyes and become its mouthpiece" (*EP*, 761/*MEW* 4, 143/*MECW* 6, 177). What is happening before their eyes, what do they place before their gaze when they become theoreticians? the active individuals: Proudhon assumes "that economic relations, viewed as immutable laws, eternal principles, ideal categories existed before acting and practicing men" (*EP*, 751/*MEW* 4, 135/*MECW* 6, 170). But on the contrary: "The same men who establish their social relations in conformity with their material productivity, produce also principles, ideas and categories in conformity with their social relations" (*EP*, 744/*MEW* 4, 130/*MECW* 6, 166). What emanates from originary production is thus complex: social relations, their theory, ideology. The 'reversal' that I spoke of finally leads to the hypostatization of social relations, theories and ideologies into giants—Prometheus, Marx says, caricaturing Proudhon: "What, then, ultimately is this Prometheus resuscitated by Mr. Proudhon? It is society, social relations based on class antagonism. These relations are not relations between individual and individual, but between worker and capitalist, between farmer and landlord, etc." (*EP*, 735/*MEW* 4, 122–123/*MECW* 6, 159).

You remember that the first product of the development of history, Marx said, was the production of new needs. Another way to state this: with the progress of civilization needs become a system. Or: the "system of needs" (*EP*, 673/*MEW* 4, 76/*MECW* 6, 119) is the systematic organization, the social relations, that both satisfies and entertains them—and even increases them. The 'system' of needs is not originary. The 'system' of needs is objectified, whereas on the level of primary needs, there is no objectification, only the struggle, with one's hands and one's body—no spiritual struggle (*H* I, 396, 401/166, 167).[120]

Anti-Humanism:
Reflections of the Turn Towards
the Post-Modern Epoch

Man is neither the oldest nor the most constant problem that has been posed for human knowledge. [...] Man is an invention of recent date. And one perhaps nearing its end.[1]

If a certain disinterest in the concept of man characterizes contemporary developments in both the human sciences and philosophy, is it possible to ascertain what deeper economy, or constellation of forces, such disinterest is a symptom of? We are told that "fundamental arrangements of knowledge" have produced the modern concept of man and that, if those arrangements were to undergo a new transmutation, "one can certainly wager that man would be erased, like a face drawn in sand at the edge of the sea."[2] I should like to look at this disinterest in man from a perspective broader than that of the archeology of the human sciences. I shall attempt to trace a displacement in the economy of words, actions and things that can be grasped only phenomenologically—if it is granted, at least, that "what must be experienced as 'the things themselves' in accordance with the principle of phenomenology" is not confined to consciousness and its objectivity,[3] but that phenomenology can afford a deconstruction of historical epochs. In a somewhat systematic fashion I want to show how in Marx, Nietzsche and Heidegger a structurally identical reversal occurs that implies more than a rearrangement in knowledge and its order, that is, more than a new *episteme*.[4] The contemporary turning away from man as the most worthwhile problem of inquiry will then appear as the symptom or manifestation of a more fundamental turning in the mode according to which things are present to speaking and acting. There is, for every epoch in history, an economy of interaction between things, gestures, and words. But this economy has not been centered on the human subject in every epoch; it has not always been, in the broadest sense of the word, humanistic. The three masters of anti-humanism, Marx, Nietzsche and Heidegger, seem to suggest that in these decades which are ours, the humanistic epochal economy is expiring.

The concept of anti-humanism, which has been in use for a decade now in so-called structuralist Marxism, polemically designates the refusal, by Marx, of a metaphysics of man as well as of the program, derived from such a metaphysics, of restoring 'integral man': in Feuerbach's terms, the program of reconciling individual man and total Man by the individual's appropriating the totality of human predicates.[5] But the concept of anti-humanism is richer than the simple polemic against idealist anthropology. It stands for an effort, in thinking, to overcome representations centered upon man in at least four different ways:

a) Cultural individuality. In this sense, the subject that anti-humanism relegates into the background of philosophy is the subject of inwardness, of the *mémoires intérieurs*; it is the inner self whose complexities fascinate Western man and which he has learned to refine through educational ideals inspired by the Renaissance, by von Humboldt and Winckelmann—or by Napoleon's *Memorial of Saint-Helena*. In a first approach, then, anti-humanism appears to be one way of conceptualizing how, with the rise of mass culture, the individual's life of the mind is threatened with homelessness.[6]

b) Reflective subjectivism. More philosophically, anti-humanism is the critique of reflection insofar as reflectivity presupposes that man can somehow draw meaning out of his own ground, that the mind only needs to take its own spontaneous acts as objects for thinking. "Reflection is nothing but an attention to what is in us."[7] Although it is the reflective subject that seems to be the *bête noire* of structuralism, a certain continuity from the former to the latter cannot be denied as soon as reflection is no longer held capable of grasping a 'thinking thing' but becomes merely a functional pole within a system of forms; that is, as soon as reflection becomes transcendental. The Kantian 'schema,' understood as an a priori multiplicity and order of functions, then appears to be the forefather of the 'structure':

c) Transcendental subjectivity. The understanding of man as a merely functional unity of a priori forms (Kant) has indeed, in its way, prepared man's elimination from the field of *episteme*. It is with Kant that man becomes questioned as the subject of the predicate 'thinking.' Transcendental subjectivity is not the counter-position to the deconstruction of the inference from thought to thinker, but on the contrary, the first step taken in the direction of that deconstruction. For the transcendental "finitude upon the basis of which we are, and think, and know,"[8] for "the system of questions commanding the answers,"[9] there are objects only in accordance with a presupposed closed functional system of variables: what Althusser calls a problematic and Foucault, an epistemic field. The 'schematic unity' of transcendentalism is thus preserved, although it is entirely dissociated from apperception. As the ego itself becomes 'subject to' such a system, the functionalism discovered with the Cogito has come to turn against it.

d) The practical subject. "History is a process, and a process without a subject."[10] When looked at from the point of view of the relations of production (Althusser) or the relations of "words and things" (Foucault), man appears as a public object, not as a private or transcendental subject. He even less appears as history-making, as a person responsible for his doings, as the initiator of a new order of things—in one phrase, as a moral agent. The old Socratic unity between knowing and doing has come apart as the subject of that unity is considered but one variable within a vast exchange of functions. It is finally the subject in this sense of an actor in history that disappears from the field of knowledge with the causality ascribed by structuralism to the combinatory organization of discourse.

These four senses of subjectivity—individuality, reflectivity, transcendentality, and morality—blend in many ways. But it is their unity that constitutes 'humanism' the way Marx, Nietzsche and Heidegger (as well as their epigones Foucault and Althusser) criticize this concept. What is identical in all three of these masters of anti-humanism and in their followers is their experience of a reversal—or rather their experience that a reversal articulates *itself through* them. I propose therefore to read them synchronically, that is, to 'cut' into the contemporary epochal economy and compare it structurally to the epoch that preceded it, the 'modern' epoch. I want to cut vertically into the post-modern constellation of things, actions and words as it appears out of one definite experience, the same in Marx, Nietzsche and Heidegger. This experience of crisis—understood literally as 'separation' (*krinein*) between epochs—is the starting point. And the claim put forward here is that this crisis allows us to examine how it is that the present economy of things, actions and words appears to be receding from man; how one can say, as Lévi-Strauss does, that man has been the "unsufferable spoiled child which has been occupying the philosophical scene far too long and has hindered all serious work by its demands for exclusive attention."[11]

Anti-humanism
A threefold break with 'humanism'

1. Althusser's characterization of the so-called epistemological break in Marx's writings is well known: "In 1845, Marx broke radically with every theory that based history and politics on an essence of man."[12] Indeed, beginning with *The German Ideology* the entire language of the human essence, borrowed directly from Feuerbach and indirectly from Hegel—although aimed against Hegel by the young Marx—disappears from Marx's thinking. Althusser indicates the following consequences of the epistemological break: a scientific theory of history and politics now becomes possible, based on such radically new concepts as "productive forces, relations to production, superstructure, ideologies, determination in the last instance by the economy," etc. Furthermore, theory can no longer be confused with philosophy, which as philosophy of consciousness is humanistic through and through. Finally, not only does philosophy appear as humanistic, but both philosophy and humanism are defined as ideology. Together they are opposed to "Marx's scientific discovery" as one field of inquiry (Althusser also says, one "continent") is opposed to another. The technical term here is "problematic." A problematic is "a typical systematic structure unifying all the elements of thought."[13] Basically there are two such problematics, the one that, in 1845, Marx turned away from, i.e., humanism, philosophy, ideology, and the one that he turned to, namely theory (political, historical, economic), science, knowledge. The turn from ideology to Marxist science is indeed one from myth to knowledge: "It is impossible to *know* anything about human beings except on the absolute precondition that the *philosophical*

myth of man is reduced to ashes."[14] Any discourse about human beings will be mythical that does not rest on the new concepts of class struggle, division of labor, ownership of means of production, etc. Such mythical discourse is opposed to science, as pure thinking is opposed to knowing. The break of 1845 is a step from thinking the essence of man, to knowing the practice of men.

Understood as the continental rift between two problematics, the ideological and the scientific, Marx's epistemological break comes about in order to last once and for all. Marx's experience of the epochal reversal from modern humanism to post-modern anti-humanism definitely draws the line between thinking and knowing. This does not mean that in the new economy of things, actions and words, there is no place for pure thinking, but that this place is the field called ideology. Non-scientific thinking will always remain, and even such thinking is necessary not only for Marxist science to clearly draft its own site of competence, but also in order to provide this science with its contents. I shall show further on that Althusser's presentation of the break is a simplification precisely insofar as it labels this break 'epistemological'; but the discovery of an anti-humanist standpoint by Marx, in 1845, is a fact. Seen from this new standpoint, his previous manuscripts appeared to him as what they are: variations on idealist humanistic themes. It seems they remained unpublished because they predated the literally 'critical' discovery of the heterogeneity between thinking and knowing.

2. A similar crisis is described by Nietzsche: "Now I shall relate the history of my *Zarathustra*. The fundamental conception of this work, the idea of the eternal recurrence, this highest formula of affirmation that is at all attainable, belongs in August 1881: it was penned on a sheet with the notation underneath, 'Six thousand feet beyond man and time.' That day I was walking through the woods along the lake of Silvaplana; at a powerful pyramidal rock not far from Surlei I stopped. It was then that this idea came to me."[15] Six thousand feet beyond man, "it" came to Nietzsche; "it invaded me," he says. The very first notation of the chief thought that Zarathustra teaches, the eternal recurrence, thus places it over and against 'man.' And the content of this teaching will be: "That everything recurs is the closest approximation of a world of becoming to a world of being: high point of the meditation."[16] In the discovery

of the eternal recurrence—here defined as convergence between becoming and being, between flux and form—culminates thinking. Prior to this invasion by something that can only be thought of, but not known, Nietzsche's philosophy was decidedly humanistic. His early writings center upon the ideal "metaphysics of the artist": an ideal of genius, of creation of values, of affirming the self against corrosive asceticism. Such affirmation, after the great discovery of 1881, is no longer the most powerful, as the text says. Only the thought of the eternal recurrence does justice to, and thus affirms, becoming—but if this thought is taken seriously, he adds, the subject appears as a fiction, as an artificial immobilization of the flux. "The 'subject' is the fiction that many similar states in us are the effect of one substratum." "My hypothesis: The subject as multiplicity."[17] This great discovery of 1881 is misunderstood as long as one does not see that it is a thought experiment with no claim to knowledge: an attempt and a temptation, he says, rather than the establishment of a hypothesis to be either verified or falsified. But if this experience of crisis is indeed *decisive*—'cutting off' one epoch from another—then there is much for us to think about, but not much to know. There are only "multiplicities in any case; but 'units' are nowhere present in the nature of becoming." There are only "complex forms of relative life-duration within the flux of becoming,"[18] only configurations of forms and forces for thinking, but no truth in and by itself. Truth, as the correlate of knowing, is itself a fiction. "Truth is the kind of error without which a certain species of life could not live."[19]

In this experience of the epochal reversal knowing and thinking are no longer assigned their respective fields, as in Marx; rather, knowing follows the fictions of thinking. "There would be nothing that could be called knowledge if thought did not first re-create the world." Knowing, then, is that fictionizing which is held to be objective, true. But from the point of view gained in 1881, truth, too, is only a thought creation, hence untrue. "Only because there is thought is there untruth."[20] And the first such untruth or fiction is 'man,' understood as the knowing and acting subject, as self.

3. The third experience of the epochal reversal of a humanistic economy to an anti-humanistic one is dated shortly before 1930. In that year culminates a development, Heidegger writes in his *Let-*

ter on Humanism, by which "everything is reversed," *"Hier kehrt sich das Ganze um."*[21] Throughout his later writings he refers to this *Kehre*, reversal or turning, as the response, in thinking, to the *Kehre* by which the economy of things, actions and words shifts into a new era. For the epochal economy, which expires in such a reversal, this change is the supreme danger: "When, in the danger, the turning comes to pass, this can happen only without mediation."[22] Abruptly, an age is no longer. To an American mind, such a sudden reversal may be understandable when one speaks of the Sixties as one order of things that has had its time. For Heidegger, such a reversal is located in thinking, again opposed to knowing and explaining. And for him, too, the type of thinking experienced in 1930 brings to an end a previous type which is as old as Western philosophy. Philosophy as a whole appears as "one thinking" to which is opposed "the other thinking," which, strictly speaking, is no longer philosophical. It is altogether a response, namely to the rise of the new epochal economy. The crisis of modernity is thus experienced as "the step back from the thinking that merely represents—that is, *explains*—to the thinking that *responds* and recalls. The step back from the one thinking to the other is no mere shift of attitude."[23] Indeed, that step is so radical that it is perilous for man's understanding of himself: "Should thinking, by means of open resistance to 'humanism,' risk a shock that could for the first time cause perplexity concerning the *humanitas* of *homo humanus* and its basis?"[24] Still more, it is perilous for man's central position in the post-modern economy: "'Humanism' now means, in case we decide to retain the word, that the essence of man is essential for the truth of being [i.e., for the epochal constellation or economy—R.S.], but in such a way that, consequently, what matters is precisely not man merely as such."[25] It is perilous even for civilization and culture: the "other thinking," the phenomenology of epochal economies, is urgent, but "not for the sake of man so that civilization and culture through man's doing might be vindicated."[26]

Marx, Nietzsche and Heidegger all set out with an interest in man: early Marxian humanism, the "metaphysics of the artist," and elucidation of existence (*Dasein*) have at least that feature in common. In all three a reversal voices itself by which the contemporary epoch properly comes into its own; by which man retreats from the scene of what is to be thought; and by which thinking gains its autonomy from knowing. These are the broad structural parallels that permit us to describe some consequences of what I called the epochal reversal towards the post-modern economy. In any case, an economy is a system. In it certain items are arranged and function according to a *nomos*, a law. These items are all those phenomena by which a given culture can be recognized. As such, they are essentially public, but they may become visible in their epochal determinateness only once their age is gone. They manifest, by their interaction, the code that rules an age. What manifests an historical order in this way is, first of all, speech. It can occur by itself, deprived of a relation to others or to things. In that case speech constitutes, not the public realm of epochal economy, but another realm, that of the text. Likewise action can occur without reference to either speech or things; togetherness is such pure action, but also the solitary invention of a theory. Finally, things may remain undealt with throughout an age; then they do not enter the exchange operated by speech and action. Defining an economy by such an interplay of speech, things and action, and following the guiding thread of the distinction between thinking and knowing, I now want to suggest how in the contemporary constellation, according to the three masters of anti-humanism, man is driven from his position as the economic principle.

The origin as manifold

When the epoch of modernity is described as the age in which subjectivity—as individuality, reflectivity, transcendentality, and morality—triumphs, this is one way of stating that since Descartes at least, but more profoundly since Plato, man is the 'principle,' the *primum captum*, in relation to which everything else comes into view. Man is the theoretical origin from whom objects receive the status of their objectivity. The very project of *mathesis universalis* is one of establishing knowledge upon the subject understood as unshakeable ground, *fundamentum inconcussum*. Knowledge is safe from the onslaught of doubt only if it rests upon a First that renders the *mathesis* precisely 'universal,' that is, 'turned towards the one.' Not so in thinking. For thinking, the origin is not a principle, but mani-fold; in thinking the word 'origin' recovers its etymological mean-ing: *oriri*, coming forth.

1. It is safe to characterize Marx's early humanism as remaining basically within the realm of a dialectic of consciousness: the uni-versal essence of man is self-alienated and, in a process of "natural-ization of man and humanization of nature," recovers its fullness of attributes. This is a realism of the universal derived from a specula-tive First, or principle, called "generic being." However—and it is here that Althusser's presentation of the "epistemological break" appears definitely simplistic—within this early problematic of uni-versals another tone rings through, which anticipates later develop-ments in Marx. A famous text, written before the break, describes the task of emancipation in Germany in the following terms: "A class must be formed which has radical chains [...] a class which is totally opposed to the premises of the German political system [...]. There must be formed a sphere of society which claims no traditional status but only a human status [...] a sphere which is the total loss of humanity and which can only redeem itself by a total redemption of humanity. This dissolution of society, as a particular class, is the proletariat."[27] The proletariat as the contradiction to the prevailing German political system *must be formed*! The class struggle is here taken out of the realm of natural dialectics and becomes the answer to the question of what must be done. Michel Henry calls this the "a priori construction of the proletariat."[28] Even more, not only is contradiction not described as a universal law in this text, but of man, too, Marx speaks otherwise than in terms of a universal essence: the "total redemption" of what is human is a practical, political goal, too. The social conditions for a conflict do not exist in Germany, Marx observes, as they do in France and England; "here is our reply," then, he says in the introduction to this text. The status of the entire Hegelian vocabulary of essence, opposition, self-alienation, universals suddenly turns from a meta-physical to a strategic one when it is used by Marx to make him-self understood by "the Germans" who only hear dialectic. This transference of contradiction and of its resolution into the realm of strategy no longer relies on any metaphysical First; it indicates a shift in what is thought of as originary.

Beginning with *The German Ideology* Marx's understanding of the origin explicitly turns away from the realism of universals and from any prime essence or subject to which individual phenomena would stand as predicates. Here, too, the key text is well-known, although not always correctly interpreted: "The premises from which we begin are not arbitrary ones, not dogmas, but real premises from which abstraction can only be made in the imagination. They are the real individuals, their activity and the material conditions of their life. [...] (Individuals) begin to distinguish themselves from animals as soon as they begin to *produce* their means of subsistence. [...] What they are, therefore, coincides with their production."[29] The new standpoint gained in 1845 is the realism of the laboring individual, expressed by the equation between reality and individual practice, and requiring that what is understood to be originary be relocated within the activity by which people sustain their living. What happens, then, in the so-called epistemological break is primarily not of an epistemological order at all. Something more fundamental occurs than the constitution of 'Marxist science.' It is the comprehension of the origin that undergoes a transmutation such that Marx can indeed claim to have put an end to all philosophies that refer the phenomenal to some noumenal in-itself, to a metaphysical *principium*.

Beginning with this break there is, properly speaking, no origin as *one* that orders the post-modern economy of things, actions and words. There is no origin, but only a profusion of originary actions by which individuals satisfy their basic needs. The origin becomes fragmented, monadic, in accordance with a monadic understanding of practice in *The German Ideology*. The 'break' must therefore be understood not only as the breaking apart of one 'continent' from the other, as the rift between ideology and science, but also as splintering, as the plurification of the origin. Within Marx's texts, the epochal reversal appears as a reversal of two problematics: the realism of universal essences, which constituted the major problematic before 1845, recedes in order to reappear later in limited theoretical fields, namely historiography, political theory, economy, and the critique of ideology. One example of such a return of the universalist realism would be the notion of 'value' in *Capital*. At the same time, in 1845, the realism of individual practice, which constituted the minor problematic in the earlier texts, comes to the fore and remains the major problematic in all philosophical works after the break—or, more precisely: it remains the philosophical background of all later writings against which alone they are correctly understood.[30] Whenever Marx speaks of universals such as classes he does so within what would have to be called regional theories, which derive their intelligibility from originary practice, the practice of the individual working in order to satisfy physical needs. Such originary practice is as irreducibly manifold as individual practices are, and it cannot be *known*. The subject-matter (such as means of production, forms of property, the classes, the state, ideologies, party strategies) of regional theories yields knowledge, but originary practice can only be *thought* of. It is quite clear that only because of his polemic against philosophy of consciousness did Marx confine thinking to ideology, understood as farthest removed from originary practice. One could depict Marx's discovery of the fragmented, plural origin according to the old scheme of the tree: originary practice would be the stem, regional theories the branches, and ideologies the extreme ramifications of that tree. Marx confines the role of thinking to these ideological ramifications; structurally, however, the matter for thinking is rather originary practice itself, the stem that holds together all theoretical knowledge. At any rate, on this basic level of originary practice no appeal is made, can be made, to the humanistic quest for self-identity, self-possession through resolution of alienation, etc. Marx's anti-humanism results, not from the discovery of a new "scientific continent" (Althusser), but from the discovery of originary practice and its monadic, atomistic allotropism.

2. A comparable fragmentation—comparable, assuredly not the same—of the origin occurs with Nietzsche's experience of thinking. Here, too, man is dislodged from his principial position as a consequence of a more radical displacement, viz., as a consequence of the transmutation of the origin as a single principle (e.g., Schopenhauer's 'will') into the origin as polymorphous activity. That in order to designate this activity Nietzsche retains the concept of will, will to power, is less important—in a sense, it is even misleading—than his declared purpose: transvaluate all values in such a way that no one of them play the role of a first principle. The

transvaluation is only a response, in thinking, to the epochal reversal that Nietzsche experienced as having placed us already in a different economy. The attempt *on* the origin as one is carried out by a historical deconstruction of how ideal truth "finally became a fable;"[31] the attempt *at* an understanding of the origin as manifold proceeds along the lines of the expression, already mentioned: "complex forms of relative life-duration within the flux of becoming." It is in this effort to think of the origin as manifold that I see the basic kinship between Marx and Nietzsche.

Nietzsche's notion of complex forms within the flux of becoming has a decidedly atomistic ring. Indeed, he acknowledges that his "way of thinking is to a great extent Heraclitean, Democritean."[32] However, instead of 'atoms,' he says 'forces.' These include cultural forces such as good and evil, but also chemical forces: "I beware of speaking of chemical 'laws' [...] it is far rather a question of the absolute establishment of power relationships."[33] The origin as manifold, then, is the ever new formation of complex forms within the flux of forces, Nietzsche calls these configurations "formations of domination." For instance: "In place of 'sociology,' a theory of the formations of domination."[34] It is this concept of formations of domination, *Herrschaftsgebilde*, which allows one to think becoming and the dissolution of the subject: "The sphere of a subject constantly growing or decreasing, the center of the system constantly shifting; in cases where it cannot organize the appropriate mass, it breaks into two parts."[35] Thus phenomena of split personalities as well as social or chemical phenomena are thought of—not 'explained,' known—in terms of such constellations of forces, "Formations of domination— the sphere of that which is dominated continually growing or periodically increasing and decreasing according to the favorability or unfavorability of circumstances."[36] These formations are aggregates of forces brought about temporarily by one more powerful force: "The individual itself as a struggle between parts (for food, space, etc.): its evolution tied to the victory or predominance of individual parts, to an atrophy, a 'becoming an organ' of other parts."[37] The concept of eternal recurrence is only one among many, in Nietzsche, to affirm such radical fluidity of inorganic, organic, social and cultural forces, all treated as equal so long as one of them does not impose its temporary order upon others.

An epochal economy of such formations of domination is by definition precarious. It corresponds entirely to the Aristotelian definition of the contingent: that which can be or not be. And yet there is no necessity other than chance, play, throwing dice to which these imperiled formations would be opposable. They are not derived from anything that might resist change. Nietzsche's program of transvaluation is the trial to overcome any representation of a First, be that man, God, a principle for reasoning or acting, or an ideal such as scientific truth. Nietzsche is assuredly entitled to the various epithets that he claims, such as Anti-Christ, Anti-Platonist, Immoralist; these names are however just so many ways of stating, not some doctrine about Christ, Plato or morality, but the foundering, at the end of modernity, of any epochal principle. They are titles for the transvaluation of the origin understood as principle into the origin understood as ever changing aggregation and disaggregation of forces into provisional economies. These economies are what is originary. Their epochal reversal occurs of itself. Once a new fold has placed us in new order, it may occur "first to one, then to many, then to all."[38] "It" occurs to some: thinking thus has nothing to do any longer with the creative deed of a genius. It becomes as anonymous as the order itself that echoes in us.

To speak of the end of a humanistic epoch thus not only implies that man is no longer the point of reference in regard to which all things can be known; it entails this deeper consequence, that man is by no means the master of the epochal economies. They unfold and fold up again. They articulate themselves in us in unforeseeable ways, and once they have had their time, the mode according to which they render things present is irretrievably lost. They arise, hold sway for a time during which they rule uncontested, and then they decline. Only after its decline can such an order be questioned. This critical questioning is what Nietzsche performs under the titles of genealogy of values and typology of the will. Values and forms of willing, his critique shows, originate in formations of domination and fall with them. So does thinking. When actions, things and words arrange themselves in a new pattern, thinking reflects their coherence and cohesion; however, it always comes like Minerva's owl, once the battle is over. What gives rise to thinking thus totally escapes our grips. Such is the discovery made by Nietzsche in that crucial summer of 1881: the anthropocentric economy, which has ruled Western culture ever since Antiquity, has revealed its perspectival nature. Any epochal principle would then be but a perspective thrown upon the chaos of forces. I take him literally when he says of this discovery: "Such is *my* experience of inspiration; I do not doubt that one has to go back thousands of years in order to find anyone who could say to me: 'It is mine as well'."[39] Thousands of years—indeed, two thousand, namely to that other caesura which instated the figure of man for the age of Western humanism. One could thus characterize the age of metaphysics as that economy which is ordered by the origin as one force, whereas "restoring innocence to becoming" would retrieve a more archaic economy in which the origin is many.

3. How does the *Kehre*, reversal or turning, displace the origin in Heidegger's thinking? The relocation that is operative here can be stated quite easily: in the writings prior to 1930, what appears as originary is human existence (*Dasein*). All phenomena are phenomena for man.—This is not the place to elaborate the differences between man as species being in the early Marx, man as creator in the early Nietzsche, and man as transcendental existence in the early Heidegger. It is only the pivotal, or referential, role played by man in these three philosophies that I want to lay bare. In Heidegger's writings before the experience of epochal reversal, the modalities of time as well as the manifold ways in which things show themselves are all referred back to man's existence and its basic structure. They are analyzed according to their "originary rootedness"[40] in existence. With the 'turning' in his thinking, on the contrary, this rootedness of phenomena in man is no longer what appears as originary. 'Origin' now comes to designate something quite different: on the one hand, the rise or incipiency of an epochal economy (*Anfang*), and on the other, the modalities in which things, words and actions are present to one another, that is, their uprise or coming to presence (*Ursprung*), within such an economy. From the first of these two points of view, we have to think of the origin as a founding event, as the beginning of an era. In this sense, thinking means remembering, recalling the nascency of an epoch. The beginning should properly be called original, not originary: in it, a constellation of truth "sets itself into work,"[41] or a world sets

itself up. Such a beginning makes everything new, produces a new arrangement, a new *nomos* of the *oikos*, a new economy. From the second point of view, that of the origin as 'uprise,' there is no event in time to be recalled. The way in which the inner arrangement of an epoch brings all that is present into an interplay, the epochal way everything has of rendering itself present: that is what must be called originary. This presence, as it prevails for a while, is something very simple; the way the Acropolis, for instance, was present within the network of actions, things and words was a definite, although complex, one when rhapsodes prepared for the Panathenaean festival; it was another when the Parthenon became a Byzantine church; still another when the Turks used it as a powder magazine; and yet another today, when UNESCO plans to spread a huge plastic cover over it to protect it from pollution. At each moment of this history the edifice was present within the order of things according to finite, unforeseeable and uncontrollable traits. And with each reversal these definite traits were irreclaimably lost.

Understood as an epochal beginning, the origin is plural. Western history is made of many such beginnings, of many "sudden epochs of truth."[42] An epoch is, properly speaking, not an era, but the event of self-instauration of an era. The word *epoche* is a term borrowed from the Stoics. In their usage, the verb *epechein* signified an act of halting, withholding, interrupting: the Stoic sage abstained from, literally 'stopped,' seeking wisdom in the midst of the many doctrines about truth in late Antiquity—and by so pausing he obtained wisdom, namely *ataraxia* or *apatheia*, equanimity. When applied to the history of fields opened and closed for life and thought, this term loses its ethical, humanistic connotation. The arrangement of what is present—Heidegger says: presenting as such—stops, punctuates, its way through the ages. There are, then, as many origins to our history as there are thresholds between periods or fields. One way of tracing these 'epochs' by which historical fields set themselves apart from one another would be to focus on the transitions in natural languages. When one begins to speak Latin instead of Greek, a new order arises; likewise, when from Latin a civilization shifts to a modern vernacular. The notion of *epoche* is thus already an anti-humanistic notion, in this context.[43] The understanding of the 'original,' i.e., of beginning, in Heidegger is quite complex, since at times he follows the German Romantics in their nostalgic return to the one great beginning of the West, preclassical Greece, and at other times he says that every work of art, even every event of speech, is its own beginning. This latter notion of beginning is expressed by the French poet, René Char: "The poet, great Beginner."[44] A beginning institutes an order that lasts or lingers for a while; furthermore, the origin as beginning is never an unshakeable, immutable first; finally, it is not a humanistic notion.

The atomization of the origin comes to completion, however, only with the understanding of the 'originary' as instantaneous uprise or encounter: "wherever a present being encounters another present being [...] a domain is opened"[45] in which things, actions and words interplay. We are to think, it seems, of such an open field as the abrupt display of the sphere in which arises whatever happens to be present. To simply think: "this or that is there," seems to be the most difficult task for thinking. Quite as for Marx and Nietzsche, the way I have proposed to read them, a reversal in thinking is required to seek what is originary nowhere else than in what is most immediately there. "The mere thought of such a task of thinking must sound strange to us. A thinking which can be neither metaphysics nor science?"[46] "Perhaps there is a thinking which is more sober than the irresistible race of rationalization. [...] Perhaps there is a thinking outside of the distinction of rational and irrational, still more sober than scientific technology, more sober and thus removed, without effect and yet having its own necessity."[47] I have tried to describe some features of this thinking: its inability to produce knowledge; its essential dependence on epochal economies, which in turn become its 'matter'; its inability to secure any ultimate ground or foundation for either metaphysical speculation or scientific investigation; and finally its denial to be at all serviceable, either as a predicate to the subject 'man' or as yielding propositions about who he is. Thinking so described would be content with gathering together whatever is there.

Thinking technology

The concept of anti-humanism has raised much hostility.[48] The point, however, is not to be 'for' or 'against' it, but to examine whether such a concept can help reveal some epochal traits of the constellation of things, actions and words as they are given today. A brief remark on the way it facilitates our thinking about technology will conclude the investigation into this concept.

Marx, critically paraphrasing Proudhon, gave a striking formulation to what I call the epochal principles: "Each principle has had its own century in which to manifest itself. The principle of authority, for example, had the eleventh century, just as the principle of individualism had the eighteenth century. Consequently, it was the century that belonged to the principle, and not the principle that belonged to the century."[49] If we take a statement like this out of the context of the polemic against idealism—that is to say, if we understand such a principle not as an in-itself—we may gather a double phenomenological truth from Marx's formulation: On the one hand it suggests how a principle, as governing a temporary network of exchanges, has its uprise, its period of reign, and its ruin, that is, how such principles are essentially precarious.[50] On the other hand it suggests that an epochal order of things can be thought of only *ex post facto*, retrospectively. It is not by chance that the examples given by Marx are taken from the past: an order of things becomes thinkable only when its temporary code expires. The economy obeyed, for a while, by the course of exploitations and the discourse of explications goes without saying while it lasts. When questions are raised in its regard, the network of exchanges that it has opened becomes confused, and a new thinking becomes possible. It seems to me that such a transition, such a blurring of epochal orders, is what shows forth in Marx, Nietzsche and Heidegger. If it is true that thinking hits upon inherent difficulties to be contemporary to its epoch—because too close, too immediately "echoing the life-process"[51]—then the primary task in its effort to understand what is called the age of technology is to return to the fold that inaugurated this age. The language of epochal economies and of anti-humanism then allows one to hold an alternative discourse about technology: from a Marxian viewpoint, the alternative

to summary labels such as 'late capitalism' would be the phenomenology of originary practice and its irreducible multifariousness;
from a Nietzschean viewpoint, the alternative to the denunciation
of technology as the "overman's" or the "master race's" global
reach (an erroneous Nietzsche interpretation, anyway) would be
the phenomenology of the will to power and its infinite modula-
tions in the formations of domination; and from a Heideggerian
viewpoint, the alternative to easy phrases about the *Gestell*, about
technological "enframing," would be the phenomenology of the
ever changing modalities of presence. In its effort to look ahead,
the 'other thinking' may then receive a hint from the description of
how the post-modern epoch arose and say with Rene Char: "That
part never fixed, asleep in us, from which will surge TOMORROW
THE MANIFOLD."[52]

This essay was first published as "Anti-Humanism: Reflections of the Turn
towards the Post-Modern Epoch," *Man and World* 12:2 (1979): 160–177.

Notes

1   [Here and in a few other instances across the lecture, Schürmann writes "eco-nomical" instead of "economic." In all subsequent instances, the adjective has been tacitly corrected.]

2   Louis Althusser, *For Marx*, trans. Ben Brewster (New York: Vintage, 1969), 24 n. [Althusser characterizes the "militant intellectuals" in the following terms: "These are real initiates, armed with the most authentic scientific and theoretical culture forewarned of the crushing reality and manifold mechanisms of all forms of the ruling ideology and constantly on the watch for them, and able in their theoretical practice to borrow—against the stream of all 'accepted truths'—the fertile paths opened up by Marx but bolted and barred by all the reigning prejudices. An under-taking of this nature and this rigour is unthinkable without an unshakeable and lucid confidence in the working class and direct participation in its struggles."]

3   [Schürmann notes "2 γ" in the margin. Possibly a reference to Aristotle, *Metaphy-sics*, trans. and ed. C.D.C. Reeve (Indianapolis and Cambridge: Hackett, 2016), Book Gamma (IV), Γ 2; 48–51, where Aristotle discusses the tasks of a science of being qua being with reference to the unicity of substance.]

4   [Schürmann notes "M. Henry" in the margin. A reference to Michel Henry (1922–2002), a French philosopher whose phenomenological interpretation of Marx serves as a crucial reference point throughout this lecture. For a more detailed discussion, see the afterword, section 2.]

5   [In the phrase "What is man?," Schürmann inserts "man" by hand for the crossed out "being."]

6   [The article "Marxist Philosophy" from the *Encyclopedia of Philosophy* is available online: https://www.encyclopedia.com/humanities/encyclopedias-almanacs-transcripts-and-maps/marxist-philosophy.]

7   Louis Althusser, "Soutenance d'Amiens," in *Positions (1964–1975)* (Paris: Éditi-ons Sociales, 1976), 127–172; 130 ["Is it simple to be a Marxist in philosophy?," in *Essays in Self-Criticism*, trans. Grahame Lock (London: NLB, 1976), 163–206; 168.]

8   [The addition "or the members of the circle around the Yugoslav periodical *Praxis* (Petrovich, Markovich, Stejanovich)" is crossed out in the manuscript but retai-ned here for the sake of the sentence's readability. Schürmann is referring to the international Western Marxist journal *Praxis*, which was published from 1964 to 1974 by the eponymous school. Founded by, among others, Gajo Petrović, Mihailo Marković and Svetozar Stojanović, it ranked among the most important interna-tional journals for Marxist theory. In the margin, Schürmann adds "W. Leonhard 350." This could be a reference to Wolfgang Leonhard, *Die Dreispaltung des Marxismus: Ursprung und Entwicklung des Sowjetmarxismus, Maoismus und Reformkommunismus* (Düsseldorf and Vienna: Econ, 1970); *Three Faces of Mar-xism: The Political Concepts of Soviet Ideology, Maoism, and Humanist Marxism*, trans. Ewald Osers (New York, Chicago and San Francisco: Holt, Rinehart and Winston, 1974), 350. In the chapter, Leonhard, a German historian who became a professor at Yale University in 1949, discusses the historical development of

"humanist marxism" in Yugoslavia and mentions the *Praxis* group. As a professor in Yale, Leonhard also provided the impetus for the first monograph on the group. See Gerson S. Sehr, *Praxis: Marxist Criticism and Dissent in Socialist Yugoslavia* (Bloomington and London: Indiana University Press, 1977), x.]

9   See Habermas' title in *Theory and Practice*: "Marxism as Critique." [Jürgen Habermas, "Between Philosophy and Science: Marxism as Critique," in *Theory and Praxis*, trans. John Viertel (Boston: Beacon Press, 1974), 195–252.]

10 [Undetermined crossing out between "These two schools […] compared." Further, Schürmann crosses out "German Ideology" and replaces it with the insertion "Althusser." Since this seems to be by mistake, the original phrasing is retained. An inequality symbol (≠) in the margin seems to further highlight the difference between the Marxist vocabulary and Schürmann's interpretation of Marx's understanding of individual practice.]

11 [In the typescript "man" is inserted by hand for the erased "being." Moreover, the phrase "being, or" before "reality" is erased as well.]

12 Herbert Marcuse, *Reason and Revolution*, 2nd ed. (London: Routledge & Kegan Paul, 1955), 273–322 ("Marx: Alienated Labor").

13 [Cited in Marcuse *Reason and Revolution*, 278–279. Marcuse glosses this as: "Labor separated from its object is, in the last analysis, an 'alienation of man from man'; the individuals are isolated from and set against each other. They are linked in the commodities they exchange rather than in their persons. Man's alienation from himself is simultaneously an estrangement from his fellow men." Marcuse, *Reason and Revolution*, 279.]

14 Hans Staudinger, "Karl Marx als ökonomischer Transzendentalphilosoph," *Die neue Zeit* 39 (1921): 453–459.

15 Michel Henry, *Marx*, 2 vols. (vol. 1, *Une philosophie de la réalité*; vol. 2, *Une philosophie de l'économie*) (Paris: Gallimard, 1976). [In collaboration with Henry, an abridged version of both volumes was translated as *Marx: A Philosophy of Human Reality*, trans. Kathleen Blamey McLaughlin (Bloomington: Indiana University Press, 1983).]

16 Kostas Axelos, *Marx, penseur de la technique: De l'aliénation de l'homme à la conquête du monde* (Paris: Les Éditions de Minuit, 1961). [Translated as: *Alienation, Praxis, and Techne in the Thought of Karl Marx*, trans. Ronald Bruzina (Austin: University of Texas Press, 1976).]

17 [Founded by Edgar Morin, Colette Audry, Roland Barthes, and Jean Duvignaud in 1956, the anti-Stalinist journal *Arguments* attracted a number of French Marxists, notably Kostas Alexos and Henri Lefebvre.]

18 [At the bottom of the typescript, Schürmann notes "Althusser" next to "constituted wholes."]

19 Herbert Marcuse, *Eros and Civilization: A Philosophical Inquiry into Freud* (Boston: Beacon Press, 1966), 149.

20 Ibid., 170.

21 Ibid., 209. [In fact, Marcuse writes "culture-building," not "culture-binding."]

22 Ibid., 210. [Here again, Marcuse writes "culture-building," not "culture-binding": "Reactivation of polymorphous and narcissistic sexuality ceases to be a threat

to culture and can itself lead to culture-building if the organism exists not as an instrument of alienated labor but as a subject of self-realization. [...]."]

23 Ibid., 236.

24 Althusser, *For Marx*, 166. [In the margin, Schürmann types the abbreviation "SK 46." The reference could not be established.]

25 See the entire section "On the Materialistic Dialectic," in Althusser, *For Marx*, 161–218.

26 Louis Althusser, *Réponse à John Lewis* (Paris: Maspero, 1972), 41. ["Reply to John Lewis," in *Essays in Self-Criticism*, 35–77; 58.]

27 [In the margin, Schürmann notes by hand: "„What is[?] man?" ie tr'[anscendent] alism > ‹ ill. › "laboring individual" > ‹ ill. ›."]

28 [This headline is crossed out in the text.]

29 Althusser, *For Marx*, 38.

30 [Schürmann marks "Kritik des Hegelschen Staatsrechts" with an "x" and notes by hand in the margin "section of philosophy of Right." Marx's manuscript *Critique of Hegel's Philosophy of the State* [*Kritik des Hegelschen Staatsrechts*] was written in the summer of 1843. It was found posthumously by David Riazanov, who published it in the *MEGA* edition in 1923. The text develops a systematic critique of §§ 261–313 of Hegel's *Outlines of the Philosophy of Right* (1820). In 1844, Marx wrote an "Introduction" for the initially planned publication of the manuscript, which was independently published in the same year under the title "A Contribution to the Critique of Hegel's Philosophy of Right: Introduction" ["Zur Kritik der Hegel'schen Rechtsphilosophie: Einleitung"]. Since most editions unite the two texts, it seems that Schürmann specifies that he refers to the *Critique of Hegel's Philosophy of the State* and not to the more programmatic introduction.]

31 [The reference is to Thomas Cooper, *Lectures on the Elements of Political Economy* (Columbia, SC: Doyle E. Sweeny, 1826), 28.]

32 [The phrase in Marx is actually *"Person Gesellschaft,"* translated as *"person-society."*]

33 [Conjecture: Schürmann inserts "philosophy of man as" by hand, but it is not entirely clear where he wanted to place the addition in the sentence.]

34 [*The Class Struggles in France* is included in the literature list given with the typescript, indicating that Schürmann might have initially planned to use this text to a greater extent than he eventually did.]

35 Marcuse, *Reason and Revolution*, 258.

36 [Schürmann is quoting from Kemp Smith's translation without indicating the edition he uses. For a recent version of the translation, see Immanuel Kant, *Critique of Pure Reason*, trans. Norman Kemp Smith (Basingstoke: Palgrave Macmillan, 2007).]

37 [Naturally, this does not take into account those of Heidegger's writings that were published since 1977. For instance, Heidegger discusses Marx in some detail in his 1969 Seminar in Le Thor, as well as in the 1973 Seminar in Zähringen. Both were first published in 1977 and are included in Martin Heidegger, *Seminare*, *Gesamtausgabe*, vol. 15, ed. Curd Ochwadt (Frankfurt am Main: Klostermann, 1986)/*Four Seminars*, trans. Andrew Mitchell and François Raffoul (Bloomington and Indianapolis: Indiana University Press, 2003).]

38 [In the margin, Schürmann adds by hand: "ie. 'break' *with* subjectivism[?]! from *particulars* to *singulars.*"]

39 [The two works Schürmann refers to are Karl Marx, *Zur Kritik der Hegelschen Rechtsphilosophie. [Kritik der Hegelschen Staatsrechts, (§§261–313)]*, MEW 1, 203–333 and *Zur Kritik der Hegelschen Rechtsphilosophie: Einleitung*, MEW 1, 378–391/*Contribution to the Critique of Hegel's Philosophy of Law*, in MECW 3, 3–129 and *A Contribution to the Critique of Hegel's Philosophy of Right: Introduction*, MECW 3, 175–187. The MECW translation diverges from the translation Schürmann is using by rendering "*Recht*" as "Law." Marx's *Critique of Hegel's Philosophy of Right* was in fact written in 1843; see above, note 30.]

40 [The original passage reads: "When the idea is made the subject [*versubjektiviert*], however, the real subjects, namely, civil society, family, 'circumstances, caprice, etc.,' become *unreal* objective elements of the idea with a changed significance."]

41 [Schürmann adds "Ritter I 965" in the margin. This most likely refers to T. Grimm's entry "Bürger, bourgeois, citoyen," in *Historisches Wörterbuch der Philosophie*, ed. Joachim Ritter, vol. 1 (Basel and Stuttgart: Schwabe & Co Verlag, 1971), 962–966.]

42 [Schürmann slightly modifies the sentence in his translation. The original reads: "The *estates* are the *posited contradiction* of the state and civil society within the state. At the same time, they are the *demand* for the *resolution* of this contradiction."]

43 [Conjecture: In the typescript, Schürmann writes "to hypostatize the general and an in-itself."]

44 [Schürmann gives as reference for this phrase *MEW* 1, 281/*MECW* 3, 77. While this phrase does not appear there literally, Marx writes that the citizen "must effect a *fundamental division* [*wesentliche Diremption*] with himself. As an *actual citizen*, he finds himself in a twofold organisation [*doppelten Organisation*]: the *bureaucratic* organisation, which is an external, formal feature of the distant state, the executive, which does not touch him or his independent reality, and the *social* organisation, the organisation of civil society."]

45 See Bertell Ollman, *Alienation: Marx's Conception of Man in a Capitalist Society* (Cambridge: Cambridge University Press, 1977); István Mészáros, *Marx's Theory of Alienation* (London: Merlin Press, 1970).

46 [Schürmann erroneously gives as reference *MEW* 1, 189, based on a misreading of the reference in *H* II, 11 n. 4. There, Henry refers to the following passage from the *Grundrisse* as an "echo" of the young Marx's philosophy of species-being: "The fact that this need on the part of one can be satisfied by the product of the other, and vice versa, and that the one is capable of producing the object of the need of the other, and that each confronts the other as owner of the object of the other's need, this proves that each of them reaches beyond his own particular need etc., as a *human being*, and that they relate to one another as human beings; that their common species-being is acknowledged by all [*daß ihr Gattungswesen von allen gewußt ist*]." (*Grundrisse der Kritik der politischen Ökonomie*, MEW 42, 168/*Grundrisse: Foundations of the Critique of Political Economy (Rough Draft)*, trans. Martin Nicolaus (London: Penguin, 1973), 243.]

47 [Karl Marx, "Debatten über das Holzdiebstahlgesetz," *MEW* 1, 109–147/"Debates on the Law on Theft of Wood," *MECW* 1, 224–263.]

48 [Typed in the margin: "Calv 79." This is most likely a reference to Jean-Yves Calvez, *La Pensée de Karl Marx* (Paris: Éditions du Seuil, 1956), 79. In this passage, Calvez discusses Marx's notion of religion as the "form of alienation itself" and elucidates how this conception is indebted to Feuerbach.]

49 [As a reference, Schürmann writes "Dietz I" without indicating a page number. The passage is actually from *The Holy Family*. Schürmann directly translates it from Henry's French citation (see *H* I, 88). The standard English translation is: "Why, then, were the consequences of the principle of self-consciousness more powerful than self-consciousness itself? Because, the answer comes after the German fashion, self-consciousness is indeed the creative principle of religious ideas [*der religiösen Vorstellungen*] but only as self-consciousness outside itself, in contradiction to itself, alienated and estranged [*außer sich gekommenes, sich selbst widersprechendes, entäußertes und entfremdetes Selbstbewußtsein*]. Self-consciousness that has come to itself, that understands itself, that apprehends its essence, therefore governs the creations of its self-alienation [*das sein Wesen erfassende Selbstbewußtsein ist daher die Macht über die Geschöpfe seiner Selbstentäußerung*]" (*MEW* 2, 42/*MECW* 3, 40–41).]

50 [Karl Marx, *Zur Judenfrage*, *MEW* 1, 347–377/*On the Jewish Question*, *MECW* 3, 146–174.]

51 [Typed in the margin: "Calv 72." This is most likely a reference to Calvez, *La Pensée de Karl Marx*, 72, who discusses the transition from the critique of religion to the critique of the state.]

52 [In the last sentence of the quote, Schürmann's modification of the English translation renders an active phrasing in the passive. The original is: "Wenn er sich zu seiner eignen Tätigkeit als einer unfreien verhält, so verhält er sich zu ihr als der Tätigkeit im Dienst, unter der Herrschaft, dem Zwang und dem Joch eines andern Menschen."]

53 [Schürmann erroneously cites the passage as stating "no more was labor." The margin has a hand-written question mark here, which might refer to the fact that the original citation is incorrect.]

54 Ludwig Feuerbach, *Das Wesen des Christentums*, in *Gesammelte Werke*, vol. 5 (Berlin: Akademie Verlag, 1975), 275 [*The Essence of Christianity*, trans. George Eliot (Walnut, CA: Mt. San Antonio College, 2008), 119.]

55 [Other translations use "[The Power of Money]" (*MECW* 3, 322), "On Money" (David McLellan, ed., *Karl Marx. Selected Writings*, 2nd ed. (Oxford: Oxford University Press, 1977), 118), or "Money" (Karl Marx, *Early Writings*, trans. Rodney Livingstone and Gregor Benton (London: Penguin, 1992), 375. The title of the section in *MEW* 40 as well as in Lieber and Furth's edition is simply "[Geld]."]

56 [Schürmann here retains the French "objectivation," while elsewhere he translates it as "objectification."]

57 [Typed in the margin: SK 39. The reference could not be established.]

58 On the historical background of Althusser's thesis, see for instance his *For Marx*, 31–39. [Schürmann adds this note in the text; it is here transformed into a footnote for readability.]

59 On these, see Althusser, *For Marx*, "Contradiction and Overdetermination," 87–128.

60 [This presumably refers to the materials published in Friedrich Engels, *Dialektik der Natur*, MEW 20, 305–570/ *Dialectics of Nature*, MECW 25, 313–619.]

61 Friedrich Engels, "Karl Marx," in David Riazanov, *Karl Marx, homme, penseur et révolutionnaire: Recueil d'articles, discours et souvenirs* (Paris: Éditions Anthropos, 1968), 12–33; 22. [*MEW* 19, 103/*MECW* 24, 192–193. Schürmann adds by hand in the margin: "date? after Marx's death †1883."]

62 Ibid., "Karl Marx," 32. [The first part of the citation could not be established. The second part (from "Our consciousness [...]") is not from Engels' "Karl Marx" but from his *Ludwig Feuerbach und der Ausgang der klassischen deutschen Philosophie*, in *MEW* 21, 259–307; 277–278/*Ludwig Feuerbach and the End of Classical German Philosophy*, in *MECW* 26, 353–398), part II, in which Engels draws out the inversion from Hegelian idealism to materialism. The full passage reads: "With irresistible force, Feuerbach is finally driven to the realisation that the Hegelian premundane existence of the 'absolute idea,' the 'pre-existence of the logical categories' before the world existed, is nothing more than a fantastic remnant of the belief in the existence of an extramundane creator; that the material sensuously perceptible world to which we ourselves belong is the only reality; and that our consciousness and thinking, however suprasensuous they may seem, are the product of a material, bodily organ, the brain. Matter is not a product of the mind, but the mind itself is merely the highest product of matter."]

63 Ibid., 84. [Schürmann seems to attribute this citation to Engels, while in fact it is taken from Lenin's "Le marxisme," in the Riazanov volume. The English translation of this text is *Karl Marx: A Brief Biographical Sketch With an Exposition of Marxism* (Peking: Foreign Languages Press, 1970), 15–16. Note that, in the English translation, Lenin refers to "Marxism," not to Marx.]

64 [Mao Tse-tung, "On Contradiction," in *Selected Works of Mao Tse-tung*, vol. 1 (Peking: Foreign Language Press, 1965), 310-347. Althusser discusses Mao's article in "Contradiction and Overdetermination," in *For Marx*, 87–128.]

65 [Typed in the margin: "Critique of the Hegelian Philosophy of Right."]

66 [Schürmann slightly modifies the sentence. The original is: "*German philosophy of law and state* is the only *German history* which is *al pari* with the official modern reality."]

67 ["Schluß des Leipziger Konzils," *MEW* 3, 437–438/"Close of the Leipzig Council," *MECW* 5, 451–452.]

68 [The original sentence is: "Where, then, is the *positive* possibility of a German emancipation?"]

69 Shlomo Avineri, *The Social and Political Thought of Karl Marx* (Cambridge: Cambridge University Press, 1968), 95.

70 Donald Hodges, "Engels' Contribution to Marxism," *Socialist Register* 2 (1965): 297–310. [Schürmann adds "Avineri p. 3 n" in the margin. The reference is to Shlomo Avineri, *The Social and Political Thought of Karl Marx*, 3 n. 2, who singles out Hodges' article.]

71 [Schürmann adds "Bruhat 17" in the margin. The reference seems to be to Jean Bruhat, *Karl Marx, Friedrich Engels: essai biographique* (Paris: Union Générale d'Éditions, 1971), 17.]

72 [Schürmann adds "ibid 66" in the margin. The reference seems to be to Bruhat, *Karl Marx, Friedrich Engels*, 66. In the 1971 edition of the book, however, it is only on page 69 that Bruhat begins to discuss Marx's time in Paris and his friendship with Engels.]

73 Shlomo Avineri, "The Hegelian Origins of Marx's Political Thought," in *Marx's Socialism*, ed. Shlomo Avineri (New York: Lieber-Atherton, 1973), 1–18; 11.

74 Ibid., 17 n. 26.

75 Avineri, *The Social and Political Thought of Karl Marx*, 3 n. 1.

76 [Schürmann adds "ibid 76" in the margin. The reference is to Bruhat, *Karl Marx, Friedrich Engels*, 76, who cites this passage from Engel's "On the History of the Communist League" on page 79. As is evident from his syntax of the phrase, Schürmann translates Engels from Bruhat's French translation. The standard English translation reads: "While I was in Manchester, it was tangibly brought home to me [*Ich war in Manchester mit der Nase darauf gestoßen worden*] that the economic facts, which have so far played no role or only a contemptible one in the writing of history, are, at least in the modern world, a decisive historical force; that they form the basis of the origination of the present-day class antagonisms; that these class antagonisms, in the countries where they have become fully developed, thanks to large-scale industry, hence especially in England, are in their turn the basis of the formation of political parties and of party struggles, and thus of all political history." See Friedrich Engels (1885), "Zur Geschichte des Bundes der Kommunisten," in *MEW* 21, 211/"On the History of the Communist League," in *MECW* 26, 317.]

77 [Schürmann adds "ibid 81" in the margin. The reference is to Bruhat, *Karl Marx, Friedrich Engels*, 81.]

78 [Schürmann adds "ibid 100" in the margin. The reference is to Bruhat, *Karl Marx, Friedrich Engels*, 100. Bruhat notes on 101 that this is a remark first made by Arnold Ruge in 1844.]

79 [Schürmann translates this citation directly from the French text in Bruhat, *Karl Marx, Friedrich Engels*, 103. The standard English translation of the entire phrase is: "When, in the spring of 1845, we met again in Brussels, Marx had already fully developed his materialist theory of history in its main features from the above-mentioned foundations, and we now applied ourselves to the detailed elaboration of the newly won outlook in the most varied directions." Friedrich Engels, "Zur Geschichte des Bundes der Kommunisten," in *MEW* 21, 212/"On the History of the Communist League," in *MECW* 26, 318.]

80 [Schürmann adds "ibid 179 s" in the margin. In accordance with the system of marginal reference used so far by Schürmann, this should be a reference to Bruhat, *Karl Marx, Friedrich Engels*, 179–180. The passage, however, does not correspond to the theme under discussion.]

81 [Schürmann adds "ibid 283" in the margin. The reference is to Bruhat, *Karl Marx, Friedrich Engels*, 283, who quotes the passage on page 282. Here again, Schürmann translates directly from the French. The passage is from Engels' letter to Johann Philipp Becker, October 15, 1884. The original can be found in *MEW* 36, 218/*MECW* 47, 202.]

82   David McLellan in his biography *Karl Marx: His Life and his Thought* (New York: Harper & Row, 1974), writes about Engels: "intellectually he had a quick, clear mind, and an ability to simplify—sometimes oversimplify—deep and complex questions" (279). "On occasion, however, Marx did criticize Engels—particularly to Jenny. After Marx's death his daughters Laura and Eleanor removed and destroyed those parts of their parents' correspondence which contained passages that might have hurt Engels." In one letter that remains, Marx "speaks in a derogatory tone of Engels himself" (280 n. 1). [This note appears near the bottom of the next page of the typescript, separated by a typed line. Since this seems to have been determined by spatial reasons alone it is placed here.]

83   Avineri, *The Social and Political Thought of Karl Marx*, 229 n. 1.

84   [Friedrich Engels, *Ludwig Feuerbach und der Ausgang der klassischen deutschen Philosophie*, in *MEW* 21, 307/*Ludwig Feuerbach and the End of Classical German Philosophy*, in *MECW* 26, 398.]

85   [The "totality of social relations" is the translation Bottomore uses to render Marx's "ensemble der gesellschaftlichen Verhältnisse" (*TF*, 68/*MEW* 3, 6).]

86   [In the typescript, Schürmann makes several handwritten additions to his initial revision of Bottomore's translation. Some minor errors occur in this process. Schürmann leaves out "reality" [*Wirklichkeit*] in the first part of the sentence, and he omits Marx's addition "not subjectively" [*nicht subjektiv*] at the end of the phrase. In the original, Marx also uses the singular genitive "des *Objekts*," not the plural. Since Schürmann works closely with this translation, it has been retained in the body of the text despite these errors. The original phrase reads: "Der Hauptmangel alles bisherigen Materialismus (den Feuerbachschen mit eingerechnet) ist, daß der Gegenstand, die Wirklichkeit, Sinnlichkeit, nur unter der Form des *Objekts oder der Anschauung* gefaßt wird; nicht aber als *sinnlich menschliche Tätigkeit, Praxis*; nicht subjektiv."]

87   [In the typescript, Schürmann deletes the last letter from his insertion of the German "Objekts." Marx's original phrasing is a genitive singular ("unter der Form des *Objekts oder der Anschauung*").]

88   [Schürmann alludes to the following passage: "What Marx recognized in an essential and significant sense, though derived from Hegel, as the estrangement of man has its roots in the homelessness of modern man. This homelessness is specifically evoked in the form of metaphysics, and through metaphysics is simultaneously entrenched and covered up as such. Because Marx by experiencing estrangement attains an essential dimension of history, the Marxist view of history is superior to that of other historical accounts." Martin Heidegger, "Brief über den 'Humanismus'," in *Wegmarken*, *Gesamtausgabe*, vol. 9, ed. Friedrich-Wilhelm v. Herrmann (Frankfurt am Main: Klostermann, 1976), 313–364; 339–340/"Letter on 'Humanism'," trans. Frank A. Capuzzi, in *Pathmarks*, ed. William McNeill (Cambridge: Cambridge University Press, 1998), 239–276; 258–259.]

89   [Schürmann seems to be quoting the preface of Hegel's *Philosophy of Right* from memory or directly from Henry's French text (see *H* I, 332). In Nisbet's translation, the entire phrase reads: "A further word on the subject of issuing instructions on how the world ought to be: philosophy, at any rate, always comes too late to perform this function [*so kommt dazu ohnehin die Philosophie immer*

zu spät]." G.W.F. Hegel, *Grundlinien der Philosophie des Rechts oder Naturrecht und Staatswissenschaft im Grundrisse*, in *Werke*, eds. Eva Moldenhauer and Karl Markus Michels, vol. 7 (Frankfurt am Main: Suhrkamp, 1986), 27–28/*Elements of the Philosophy of Right*, trans. H. B. Nisbet, ed. Allen W. Wood (Cambridge: Cambridge University Press, 1991), 23.]

90 [Schürmann omits here the beginning of the phrase. In Nisbet's translation: "As the *thought* of the world, it appears only at a time when actuality has gone through its formative process and attained its completed state [*nachdem die Wirklichkeit ihren Bildungsprozeß vollendet und sich fertig gemacht hat*]." Hegel, *Grundlinien der Philosophie des Rechts*, 28/*Elements of the Philosophy of Right*, 23.]

91 Althusser, *For Marx*, 166.

92 [In this and the following lecture, Schürmann frequently cites a passage from the chapter "The Determination of Reality" from Henry's *Marx* that is not included in the English translation.]

93 [The beginning of the sentence has been slightly modified for readability. Schürmann writes: "At the same time are abandoned phrases [...]".]

94 [Schürmann adds "Nachw 885 ff" in the margin. The reference is to Hans Joachim Lieber and Peter Furth, "Nachwort," in *Werke–Schriften*, vol. 2, *Frühe Schriften*, ed. Hans Joachim Lieber and Peter Furth (Darmstadt: Wissenschaftliche Buchgesellschaft, 1971), 885–890. Schürmann quotes *The German Ideology* from this volume of Lieber and Furth's edition, which was the first to take a critical stance towards the preceding editions (i.e., the Landshut and Mayer edition as well as the first *MEGA* edition and the subsequent *MEW* editions published by Dietz Verlag), based upon a reexamination of the manuscripts. The main divergences concern the so-called Feuerbach chapter as well as the headlines. However, in what follows, Schürmann does occasionally refer to those older headlines that Furth and Lieber eliminated from their edition.]

95 [Schürmann notes "McLellan, p 207 f." The reference appears to be to McLellan, *Karl Marx*, 207–208, but the author does not address the theme in the indicated passage. However, McLellan does comment on Marx and Engels' practice of writing manuscripts as a way of self-clarification on page 29 and with explicit reference to *The German Ideology* on 151–152.]

96 [Karl Marx, *Zur Kritik der Politischen Ökonomie*, in *MEW* 13, 10/*Outlines of the Critique of Political Economy*, *MECW* 29, 264].

97 [Marx's letter to Kugelmann from April 24, 1867. See *MEW* 31, 290/*MECW* 42, 360.]

98 Friedrich Engels, *Ludwig Feuerbach und der Ausgang der klassischen deutschen Philosophie*, in *MEW* 21, 264/*Ludwig Feuerbach and the End of Classical German Philosophy*, in *MECW* 26, 359.

99 [The "German editors" refers to Hans Joachim Lieber and Peter Furth. See footnote 94.]

100 [Schürmann gives no reference for this passage, which is probably due to the fact that he translates it directly from Henry's French quotation (*H* I, 352). The standard English translation of the passage is: "This manner of approach is not devoid of premises. It starts out from the real premises and does not abandon them for a moment. Its premises are men, not in any fantastic isolation and fixity,

but in their actual, empirically perceptible process of development under definite conditions. As soon as this active life-process is described, history ceases to be a collection of dead facts, as it is with the empiricists (themselves still abstract), or an imagined activity of imagined subjects, as with the idealists" (*MEW* 3, 27/*MECW* 5, 37).]

101 [All subsequent references in this paragraph are to this section. The *MEW* edition does not include the respective heading.]

102 [As the *MEW* edition specifies, the phrase is placed in a footnote because it was crossed out in the manuscript. Also see Furth and Lieber's editorial note in *DI*, 15–16 n. 3.]

103 [Schürmann adds "(footnote)" as a reference. Here again, the passage appears in the footnote because it was crossed out in the manuscript.]

104 [Schürmann gives no reference for this quote. Presumably, he has in mind the following phrase on "real individuals": "What they are, therefore, coincides with their production, both with *what* they produce and with *how* they produce" (*DI*, 17/*MEW* 3, 21/*MECW* 5, 31–32).]

105 [In the typescript, Schürmann underlines the definitive article "*die*" in "*die Arbeit*" to emphasize the theoretical status of labor conceived as a universal.]

106 [Conjecture: In the typescript, Schürmann writes after the colon "this the division of labor is the genealogical origin of social formations."]

107 [In the original: "We have already shown above that the abolition of a state of affairs in which relations become independent of individuals, in which individuality is subservient to chance and the personal relations of individuals are subordinated to general class relations, etc.—that the abolition of this state of affairs is determined in the final analysis by the abolition of division of labour [*der Subsumtion ihrer persönlichen Verhältnisse unter die allgemeinen Klassenverhältnisse etc. in letzter Instanz bedingt ist durch die Aufhebung der Teilung der Arbeit*]."]

108 [In the left margin, Schürmann writes "confér. Lefort." This is presumably a reference to a conference presentation by Claude Lefort. While it could not be established whether he presented it at a conference, Lefort, in an essay published one year after Schürmann gave this lecture, discusses different visions of history in Marx's work. See Claude Lefort, "Marx: d'une vision de l'histoire à l'autre," in *Les Formes de l'histoire: essais d'anthropologie politique* (Paris: Gallimard, 1978), 195–233/"Marx: From One Vision of History to Another," trans. Terry Kartell, in *The Political Forms of Modern Society: Bureaucracy, Democracy, Totalitarianism*, ed. John B. Thompson (Cambridge, MA: MIT Press, 1986), 139–180. We would like to thank Peg Birmingham and Christiane Frey for elucidating this reference.]

109 [Marx and Engels, *Das kommunistische Manifest*, in *MEW* 4, 462/*Communist Manifesto*, in *MECW* 6, 482.]

110 [Ibid., 463/485.]

111 [Ibid., 467/489.]

112 [Marx, *Grundrisse*, in *MEW* 42, 383/*Grundrisse: Foundations of the Critique of Political Economy*, 471. The English translation renders "natürliches Laboratorium" as "natural workshop."]

113 [Schürmann crosses out this whole section by hand. Parts of its content are repeated in the first paragraph of the subsequent Chapter 8.]

114 [Schürmann substitutes "But he" for "The youth as a man" in the citation.]

115 [Schürmann modifies the translation, replacing an active with a passive phrase. The *MECW* translation is: "[…] which we have assembled […]."]

116 [The letter to Franz Mehring that Schürmann here erroneously attributes to Marx was in fact written by Friedrich Engels in London on July 14, 1893, more than ten years after Marx's death. Schürmann modifies the sentence composition; the *MECW* translation reads: "The actual motives by which he is impelled remain hidden from him, for otherwise it would not be an ideological process." In the margin, Schürmann notes "Dico," a common abbreviation for dictionary in French and possibly Schürmann's source for this citation. Which dictionary he might be referring to could not be established.]

117 Althusser, *For Marx*, 183.

118 [Schürmann gives as reference "Dtsch I, 426," based on the citation of the passage in Henry's book. However, the latter quotes not from the German original (which the abbreviation "Dtsch" seems to indicate), but from the French translation by Roger Dangeville, *Grundrisse: Fondements de la critique de l'économie politique* (Paris: Éditions Anthropos, 1967), vol. 1, 426. See *MEW* 42, 375/*Grundrisse: Foundations of the Critique of Political Economy*, 463. Dangeville shifts the sentence structure from constative to conditional. The—more literal—English translation reads: "The recognition [*Erkennung*] of the products as its own, and the judgement that its separation from the conditions of its realization is improper and forcibly imposed—is an enormous [advance in] consciousness [*Bewusstsein*] […]" (translation modified). In the sentence preceding the cited passage, Marx describes the expenditure of labor-time as the expenditure of "life forces [*ausgegebne Lebenskraft*]," which Dangeville translates as "force vitale" and which Schürmann might have taken to be another indicator of the vitalist moment in Marx's critique of political economy. We would like to thank Antoine Hummel for his help in establishing this reference.]

119 Althusser, *For Marx*, 244.

120 [Under the last line of the typed text, Schürmann adds by hand: "Dognin, pp. 94 ‹ ill. ›." The reference is probably to Paul-Dominique Dognin, *Initiation à Marx* (Paris: Les Éditions du Cerf, 1970). Father Paul-Dominique Dognin was one of Schürmann's erstwhile teachers, see the afterword. Schürmann also adds by hand: "Conclusion: anti-Hum article"—referring to the essay that is reprinted in this volume. At the bottom of the page, Schürmann notes: "Später mal: Bd II !!," which translates as "another time:" or "later on: vol. 2!!" This is the only marginal note in German in the lecture and it possibly indicates that Schürmann planned to engage in more detail with the second volume of Henry's work on Marx, which is dedicated to the economic writings. We would like to thank Francesco Guercio for his help in deciphering this annotation.]

Anti-Humanism: Reflections of the Turn Towards the Post-Modern Epoch

1   Michel Foucault, *The Order of Things: An Archaeology of the Human Sciences*, trans. Alan M. Sheridan (New York: Vintage Books, 1973), 386–387.

2   Ibid. [Foucault, *The Order of Things*, 387.]

3   Martin Heidegger, *On Time and Being,* trans. Joan Stambaugh (New York: Harper & Row, 1972), 79 ["Mein Weg in die Phänomenologie," in *Zur Sache des Denkens*, *Gesamtausgabe*, vol. 14 (Frankfurt am Main: Klostermann, 2007), 99. Subsequent references to this edition are abbreviated as *"GA,"* followed by the number of the volume.]

4   See the description of this epistemic region as "always more solid, more archaic, less dubious, always more 'true' than the theories […]." Foucault, *The Order of Things*, xvi.

5   Louis Althusser, *For Marx*, trans. Ben Brewster (New York: Vintage, 1969), 229. Later, in *Reading Capital*, trans. Ben Brewster (New York: Random House, 1970), 119, he corrects himself: "I ought to say an a-humanism," in order to indicate, not only the theoretical negation of humanism, but the sheer absence of any reference to it in scientific Marxism. In *Positions* (Paris: Éditions sociales, 1976), 132, however, he speaks again of anti-humanism.

6   Foucault, *The Order of Things*, 343. In Foucault's diatribe against "all those who still wish to talk about man, about his reign or his liberation, all those who still ask themselves questions about what man is in his essence, all those who wish to take him as their starting-point in their attempts to reach the truth, all those who, on the other hand, refer all knowledge back to the truths of man himself, all those who refuse to formalize without anthropologizing, who refuse to mythologize without demystifying, who refuse to think without immediately thinking that it is man who is thinking" (ibid., 342–343), it is safe to say that the concept of man is not exactly univocal. [The location of this endnote is a conjecture. Although it appears as an endnote in Schürmann's article, the corresponding reference—note number six—does not appear in the body of the text.]

7   Gottfried W. Leibniz, "New Essays on the Human Understanding," Preface, No. 4, in *Philosophical Writings,* trans. Mary Morris (London: J. M. Dent & Sons, 1934), 146. The 'humanistic' essence of reflection does not change, of course, when reflection is said to be 'concrete,' when it is defined as "the appropriating of our effort to exist." Paul Ricœur, *Freud and Philosophy: An Essay on Interpretation,* trans. D. Savage (New Haven: Yale University Press 1970), [46]; see also 56 and 494–495. [The page reference for the quote is missing in Schürmann's article, as is the emphasis in the original. The additional reference "see also 56 and 494–495" is Schürmann's.]

8   Foucault, *The Order of Things*, 375.

9   Althusser, *For Marx*, 67 n. 30. [Schürmann omits the emphasis which Althusser places on *"questions"* and *"answers."*]

10   Louis Althusser, *Réponse à John Lewis* (Paris: Maspero, 1972), 31. ["Reply to John Lewis," in *Essays in Self-Criticism,* trans. Grahame Lock (London: NLB, 1976), 51. Schürmann omits the emphasis which Althusser places on *"process without a subject."*]

11 Claude Lévi-Strauss, *L'homme nu* (= *Mythologica* IV) (Paris: Plon, 1971), 614–615. [*The Naked Man: Introduction to a Science of Mythology 4*, trans. John and Doreen Weightman (London: Jonathan Cape, 1981), 687.]

12 Althusser, *For Marx*, 227.

13 Ibid., 67.

14 Ibid., emphasis added.

15 Friedrich Nietzsche, *Ecce Homo*, 'Thus Spoke Zarathustra,' 1, *Basic Writings*, trans. and ed. Walter Kaufmann, (New York: Modern Library, 1966), 731 [*Ecce Homo, Kritische Studienausgabe*, ed. Giorgio Colli and Mazzino Montanari, vol. 6 (Berlin: de Gruyter, 1999), 335. Subsequent references to this edition are abbreviated as "*KSA*," followed, first, by the number of the volume, then (if applicable) by the number of the aphorism and, finally, by the page number.]

16 Friedrich Nietzsche, *The Will to Power*, sect. 617, trans. Walter Kaufmann (New York: Random House, 1968), 330. [*KSA* 12, 7[54], 312.]

17 Ibid., sects. 485 and 490; 269–270. [*KSA* 12, 10[19], 465.]

18 Ibid., sect. 715, 580. [*KSA* 13, 11[73], 36.]

19 Ibid., sect. 493, 272. [*KSA* 11, 34[253], 506. In the *KSA* edition, the first part of the sentence is in italics *"Truth is the kind of error […]."*]

20 Ibid., sect. 574, 309. [*KSA* 10, 8[25], 343.]

21 Martin Heidegger, ["Letter on Humanism," in] *Basic Writings*, ed. David F. Krell (New York: Harper & Row 1977), 208. ["Brief über den Humanismus," in *Wegmarken (1919–1961)*, GA 9, 328.]

22 Martin Heidegger, ["The Turning," in] *The Question Concerning Technology*, trans. W. Lovitt (New York: Harper & Row 1977), 44. ["Die Kehre," in *Identität und Differenz (1955–1957)*, GA 11, 120.]

23 Martin Heidegger, ["The Thing," in] *Poetry, Language, Thought*, trans. Albert Hofstadter (New York: Harper & Row, 1971), 281. Emphases added. ["Das Ding," in *Vorträge und Aufsätze (1936–1953)*, GA 7, 183.]

24 Heidegger, ["Letter on Humanism," in] *Basic Writings*, 225. ["Brief über den Humanismus," GA 9, 346.]

25 Ibid., 224. The translation by F.A. Capuzzi is erroneous here. [Heidegger's phrasing is "daß es demzufolge gerade nicht auf den Menschen, lediglich als solchen, ankommt." See "Brief über den Humanismus," GA 9, 345.]

26 Ibid., 209. ["Brief über den Humanismus," GA 9, 329.]

27 Karl Marx, *Critique of Hegel's Philosophy of Right*, ed. Joseph O'Malley, trans. Annette Jolin (Cambridge: Cambridge University Press, 1970), 141–142; translation slightly modified. [*MEW* 1, 390/*MECW* 3, 186.]

28 Michel Henry, *Marx*, 2 vols. (Paris: Gallimard, 1976), vol. I, 136. [*Marx: A Philosophy of Human Reality*, trans. Kathleen Blamey McLaughlin (Bloomington: Indiana University Press, 1983), 63.] In the interpretation of the 'break' that follows, as well as for the notion of originary practice, I am partly indebted to these two volumes.

29 Karl Marx and Friedrich Engels, *The German Ideology*, trans. Clemens Dutt, W. Lough and C.P. Magill (Moscow: Progress Publishers, 1976), 36–37. [*MEW* 3, 20–21/*MECW* 5, 31.]

30 The realism of universals comes to prevail again in Engels and in Marxism as a whole, particularly Althusser's, according to Michel Henry; see Henry, *Marx*, vol. I, 25, 220, 318–321, 348–349, 373, 379, 405, 426–427, 461–466. [The majority of these critical passages on Althusser are missing from the abridged English translation. Those that are included can be found in Henry, *Marx*, 11, 141–142, 161, 163.]

31 Friedrich Nietzsche, *Twilight of the Idols*, "How the 'True World' Finally Became a Fable," in *The Portable Nietzsche*, trans. and ed. Walter Kaufmann (New York: The Viking Press, 1954), 485 [*Götzendämmerung*, "Wie die 'wahre Welt' endlich zur Fabel wurde," *KSA* 6, 80]. This text traces six epochs (Nietzsche also says "punctuations," which is a literal translation of *epechein*, halting, stopping) of a deconstruction of metaphysics understood as an ontology of the "ideal world."

32 Nietzsche, *Will to Power*, sect. 428, 233. [*KSA* 13, 14[116], 293.]

33 Ibid., sect. 630, 336. [*KSA* 11, 36[18], 559.]

34 Ibid., sect. 462, 255. [*KSA* 12, 9[8], 342.]

35 Ibid., sect. 488, 270. [*KSA* 12, 9[98], 391–392.]

36 Ibid., sect. 715, 380. [*KSA* 13, 11[73], 36.]

37 Ibid., sect. 647, 344. [*KSA* 12, 7[25], 304.]

38 Friedrich Nietzsche, *Die Unschuld des Werdens*, vol. II, sect. 1332 (Stuttgart: Kröner, 1965), 473. [*KSA* 9, 11[148], 498.]

39 Nietzsche, *Ecce Homo*, "Thus Spoke Zarathustra," n. 3, in *Basic Writings*, 757. [*Ecce Homo*, "Also sprach Zarathustra," *KSA* 6, 340.]

40 Martin Heidegger, *Being and Time*, trans. John Macquarrie and Edward Robinson (New York: Harper, 1962), 429. The phrase is poorly translated, see 377 of the German original. [The original phrase is "*ursprünglichen Verwurzelung*," Martin Heidegger, *Sein und Zeit* (Tübingen: Max Niemeyer Verlag, 1967), 377.]

41 Heidegger, ["The Origin of the Work of Art," in] *Poetry, Language, Thought*, 61. ["Der Ursprung des Kunstwerks," in *Holzwege*, *GA* 5, 50.]

42 Heidegger, ["Nietzsche's Word: 'God Is Dead'," in] *The Question Concerning Technology*, 54. ["Nietzsches Wort 'Gott ist tot'," in *Holzwege*, *GA* 5, 210.]

43 The *epoche* so understood implies an imperative: "to transform our accustomed ties to world and earth and henceforth to restrain from all usual doing and prizing, knowing and looking," *Poetry, Language, Thought*, 64 ["Der Ursprung des Kunstwerks," in *Holzwege*, *GA* 5, 54]. This "restraining," *an sich halten*, recalls directly Cicero's advice to "withhold one's assent," *Academica*, II, 59 [*De Natura Deorum, Academica*, trans. and ed. Harris Rackham (Cambridge, MA: Harvard University Press, 1967), 543], as well as that of Sextus Empiricus, to "reserve oneself with regard to all things," *epechein peri panton, Hypotyposes*, I, 232–233 [*Outlines of Scepticism*, trans. and ed. Jonathan Barnes (Cambridge: Cambridge University Press, 2000), 61–62]. Nietzsche seems to anticipate Heidegger's notion of *epoche* when he *speaks* of "punctuations" [*"Punktationen"*] of the "centers of domination," *The Will to Power*, sect. 715, 380 [*"Herrschafts-Gebilde*," *KSA* 13, 11[73], 36]. In a footnote to this text the translator acknowledges his inability to understand the concept of 'punctuation' and consequently mistranslates it as "treaty drafts"!

44 René Char, *Fureur et mystère* (Paris: Gallimard, 1962), 83.

45 Heidegger, ["The End of Philosophy and the Task of Thinking," in] *On Time and Being*, 64. ["Das Ende der Philosophie und die Aufgabe des Denkens," *GA* 14, 80.]
46 Ibid., 59. [*GA* 14, 74.]
47 Ibid., 72. [*GA* 14, 89.]
48 The concept of anti-humanism has been opposed most vehemently by the French 'Personalists,' the disciples of Emmanuel Mounier, mainly Mikel Dufrenne, Paul Ricœur and the journal *Esprit*; see the special issues of the latter of November, 1963, May, 1967, March, 1973. See also Mikel Dufrenne, *Pour l'homme* (Paris: Seuil, 1968), and Paul Ricœur's long review of Michel Henry's interpretation in *Esprit* 2:10 (1978): 124–139. [The text is titled "Le 'Marx' de Michel Henry."]
49 Karl Marx, *The Poverty of Philosophy*, trans. Frida Knight (New York: International Publishers, 1963), 115. [*MEW* 4, 134/*MECW* 6, 170. The translation has been modified by Schürmann.]
50 See my "Principles Precarious: On the Origin of the Political in Heidegger," in *Martin Heidegger: The Man and the Thinker*, ed. Thomas Sheehan (Chicago: Precedent Publishing, 1981), 245–256. [In the original version of Schürmann's essay, this reference is marked as 'forthcoming'.]
51 Marx and Engels, *The German Ideology*, 42. [*MEW* 3, 26/*MECW* 5, 36. The translation has been modified by Schürmann.]
52 "Cette part jamais fixée, en nous sommeillante, d'où jaillira DEMAIN LE MULTIPLE," René Char, *Commune présence* (Paris: Gallimard, 1964), 255.

Afterword

On Transcendental Materialism: Reiner Schürmann's Reading of Marx

Malte Fabian Rauch and Nicolas Schneider

1. Introduction

On the final page of the typescript of this lecture course, under the very last line of text, Schürmann notes by hand "Dognin, pp. 94 ‹ ill. ›."[1] The reference is probably to a book by Paul-Dominique Dognin, *Initiation à Marx*. Father Dognin was one of Schürmann's teachers at *Le Saulchoir* in Étiolles, the convent school outside of Paris where he undertook most of his earlier studies. In the passages that Schürmann seems to be pointing to, Dognin elaborates on the relation between the human being and nature in Marx's work.[2] In the first part, Dognin distinguishes Marx's analysis of this relation in the *Economic and Philosophic Manuscripts of 1844* from that found in his later works, observing that, while in the *Manuscripts* Marx focuses on the alienation of the human being from itself, the later writings prioritize the antagonism between different social groups. In the section that follows, Dognin traces the inversion of the Hegelian dialectic through Feuerbach and Marx,

---

1   In this volume, 95 n. 120. We would like to thank Kieran Aarons for his comments on a draft version of this afterword.

2   Paul-Dominique Dognin, *Initiation à Marx* (Paris: Les Éditions du Cerf, 1970), 94–95 and 95–101, respectively. Dognin also published a French translation and commentary of the first chapter of Marx's *Capital*. See *Les "sentiers escarpés" de Karl Marx*, 2 vols. (Paris: Les Éditions du Cerf, 1977). The materials kept at the New School archive suggest that, in the winter of 1964–1965, Schürmann attended a course delivered by Dognin on Marx and his philosophical predecessors that was divided into two parts, the first more general on "Social Philosophy" (it lists Auguste Comte, Ludwig Feuerbach, Aristotle, Aquinas, Hegel, Max Stirner), the second on "Marxism" in particular. See Reiner Schürmann, *Reiner Schürmann Papers, 1958–1993*, The New School Archives and Special Collections (New York: The New School), NA.0006.01, box 1, folder 29.

noting that, beginning with the *Manuscripts*, Marx transposes the dialectic from a deistic into an atheistic totality, in which the overcoming of alienation is tantamount to the human being's reconciliation with nature. The background presence of Dognin's interpretation elucidates Schürmann's sustained engagement with Marx in the development of his thought.

"Reading Marx": the title of the lectures is not only a polemic against Louis Althusser; it also betrays an affinity to Maurice Blanchot's text "Lire Marx." Blanchot distinguishes three voices in Marx—a philosophical, a political and a scientific one—that interlace and disrupt one another, creating a "communist voice that is always *at once* tacit and violent, both political and scholarly, direct, indirect, total and fragmented, long and almost instantaneous."[3] Bearing witness to a similar sensibility, the reading of Marx offered in this 1977 lecture course reflects the persistence of Schürmann's engagement with the critique of political economy, but it also marks a turning point when compared with his own earlier interpretations of Marx.[4] What one encounters here, as well as in the 1979 essay, "Anti-Humanism: Reflections of the Turn towards the Post-Modern Epoch," which Schürmann suggested as the conclusion of the lecture course,[5] is the emergence of the forceful reading that would become a constitutive element of his first major work, *Le principe d'anarchie: Heidegger et la question de l'agir*, published in 1982. There, Marx is inscribed in a genealogy that Schürmann terms "A Threefold break with 'Humanism'." While this constellation is only hinted at in this lecture course when he juxtaposes

---

3   Maurice Blanchot, "Lire Marx," *Comité* 1 (October 1968): 31; reprinted as "Les trois paroles de Marx," in *L'amitié* (Paris: Gallimard, 1971), 115–117; 117/"Marx's Three Voices," trans. Tom Keenan, in *Friendship*, trans. Elizabeth Rottenberg (Stanford: Stanford University Press, 1997), 98–100; 100.

4   See, for instance, the references to Marx, as well as the epigraph by Gramsci, in an article from the year prior to this lecture course. Reiner Schürmann, "La praxis symbolique," *Cahiers Internationaux de Symbolisme* 29/30 (1976): 145–170/"Symbolic Praxis," trans. Charles T. Wolfe, *Graduate Faculty Philosophy Journal* 19:2/20:1 (1997): 39–65. This essay will be re-published in Reiner Schürmann, *The Place of the Symbolic: Essays on Art and Politics*, eds. Malte Fabian Rauch and Nicolas Schneider (Zurich: Diaphanes, forthcoming).

5   In this volume, 95 n. 120.

Marx's thinking of "being as irreducibly manifold" to the thought of Nietzsche and Heidegger, it takes center stage in the "Anti-Humanism" article, which actually is a draft of the respective section in *Le principe d'anarchie*.[6]

In the work of Marx, Nietzsche and Heidegger, Schürmann contends, one can observe a rupture "through which the operative concept of origin ceases to be humanistic and becomes plural," or, in his more technical terms, a "transition from a principial economy to an anarchic economy of presence."[7] What their philosophies afford are a perspective on the 'originary' or 'primary needs' that, in the history of Western philosophy, become objectified into a principial economy or, in Marx's terms, "a system of needs." This is what Schürmann points to in the very last paragraph of the lectures when citing Henry's phrase of "the struggle, with one's hands and one's body—no spiritual struggle."[8] In Schürmann's vocabulary, the "origin" or "*arche*" denotes a metaphysical foundation that dominates an epoch by externally imposing unity and sense on all actions. Seen in this perspective, Marx, Nietzsche and Heidegger oppose

---

6   In this volume, 100–104, and Reiner Schürmann, *Le principe d'anarchie: Heidegger et la question de l'agir* (Bienne and Paris: Diaphanes, 2013)/*Heidegger on Being and Acting: From Principles to Anarchy*, trans. Christine-Marie Gros (Bloomington: Indiana University Press, 1987), § 7.

7   Ibid., 63–64/44–45. It is reasonable to assume that Schürmann, a careful reader of Ricœur, conceived this triumvirate of anti-humanism in dialogue with Ricœur's famous three "masters of suspicion" (Marx, Nietzsche, Freud). See Paul Ricœur, *Freud and Philosophy: An Essay on Interpretation*, trans. D. Savage (New Haven: Yale University Press 1970), 32–36. And it is almost certain that Schürmann developed this genealogy of "anti-humanism" in opposition to Jacques Derrida's interpretation of the equivocality of the end of humanism as "the play of *telos* and death." See Jacques Derrida, "The Ends of Man," in *Margins of Philosophy*, trans. Alan Bass (Chicago: University of Chicago Press, 1982), 109–136; 134.

8   And while Schürmann, as the marginal note on the last page of the typescript indicates, planned to undertake an engagement with Marx's economic writings, he ultimately avoided this confrontation. It is possible that such a confrontation would have necessitated a revision of the claim that the notion of value that Marx elaborates in *Capital* reintroduces a realism of universals. For an attempt to situate Schürmann's 'epochal' notion of "economy" in a genealogy of the term that traces its development from a theological to a financial term, see Giorgio Agamben, *The Kingdom and the Glory: For a Theological Genealogy of Economy and Government* (Homo Sacer II, 2), trans. Lorenzo Chiesa (Stanford: Stanford University Press, 2011), 64–65.

the hegemonic ontologies of Western philosophy by suspending the traditional mode of relating theory to practice, in which the former provides the principle—the *arche*—for the latter to execute. In their work, the subject appears as merely the last of a series of such strategies that aim to ground action in a *prima philosophia*. And since the subject is the ultimate *arche*, the understanding of being as "irreducibly manifold"—that is, as difference—necessarily articulates itself as a break with "humanism." Anti-foundationalism necessitates anti-humanism, and vice versa.

Accordingly, what makes Marx's thinking so important for Schürmann in this lecture is the "radical novelty" he sees in "the equation between *praxis* and *being*,"[9] together with the disenchanted insight that those who have claimed Marx's legacy have relapsed into ways of thinking that betray their ignorance of the scope of Marx's philosophical critique. While Schürmann is adamant that what matters is Marx's "philosophical axis,"[10] it should be clear that its stakes are of more than mere scholarly concern; rather, Schürmann's reading of Marx must be seen as an original attempt to respond to the challenges arising from the cycle of revolutionary struggles spreading across the world since the late 1960s. As such, Schürmann's lecture course can be situated among a series of phenomenological and deconstructive projects in the 1970s—such as those of Jacques Derrida, Michel Henry, and Gérard Granel—that sought to develop philosophical readings of Marx at variance with official Marxism and in response to the new political situation.[11]

---

9   In this volume, 18.

10   In this volume, 13–14.

11   Since the late 1960s, Gérard Granel developed a Heideggerian reading of Marx that also centers on a theory of "being as production" in contradistinction to Althusser's epistemological interpretation. See Gérard Granel (1969), "Incipit Marx: l'ontologie marxiste de 1844 et la question de la 'coupure'," in *Traditionis traditio* (Paris: Gallimard, 1972), 179–230. Jacques Derrida's seminar on *Theory and Praxis* is contemporaneous with Schürmann's lecture course and also engages with the constellation of Heidegger, Marx, and Althusserian structuralism. See Jacques Derrida, *Théorie et pratique: Cours de l'ENS-Ulm 1975–1976*, ed. Alexander García Düttmann (Paris: Galilée, 2017)/*Theory and Praxis*, eds. Geoffrey Bennington and Peggy Kamuf, trans. David Wills (Chicago and London: University of Chicago Press, 2019).

2. Constellation and conjuncture

In the first lecture, Schürmann frames his interpretation methodologically by noting that he seeks to situate Marx within the "Heideggerian 'Destruction of the History of Ontology'."[12] Even though Heidegger himself did not develop such a reading of Marx, Schürmann argues, "the Heideggerian presuppositions coincide here with the basic turn of the decisive philosophical texts after 1845."[13] This deceptively modest proposition conceals the radical divergence of Schürmann's interpretation of Marx from that of Heidegger, which nonetheless is crucial for understanding the direction of this lecture. As is well known, Heidegger, too, positions Marx at the end of metaphysics, but he does so in an altogether different way: "With the reversal [*Umkehrung*] of metaphysics, which was already accomplished by Karl Marx, the outmost possibility of philosophy is attained."[14] According to this reading, metaphysics reveals itself, in its final gathering, as the "technology of man." Marx's materialism, Heidegger asserts, consists "in a metaphysical determination according to which every being appears as the material of labor," a determination that is said to have been anticipated in Hegel as the "self-establishing process of unconditioned production."[15] By contrast, on Schürmann's reading, Marx's materialism does not fulfil metaphysics, but begins to dislocate its ground, a metamorphosis that anticipates Heidegger's own project precisely through those concepts he had denigrated as metaphysical: subject, labor, production.

The central tenet of Schürmann's reading is that Marx develops a new conception of transcendental subjectivity, whose constitutive

---

12   In this volume, 21.

13   In this volume, 22.

14   Martin Heidegger, "Das Ende der Philosophie und die Aufgabe des Denkens," in *Zur Sache des Denkens, Gesamtausgabe*, vol. 14, ed. Friedrich-Wilhelm von Herrmann (Frankfurt am Main: Klostermann, 2007), 67–90; 71/"The End of Philosophy and the Task of Thinking," in *On Time and Being*, trans. Joan Stambaugh (New York: Harper & Row, 1972), 55–73; 57. Translation modified.

15   Martin Heidegger, "Brief über den 'Humanismus'," in *Wegmarken, Gesamtausgabe*, vol. 9, ed. Friedrich-Wilhelm von Herrmann (Frankfurt am Main: Klostermann, 1976), 313–364; 340/"Letter on 'Humanism'," trans. Frank A. Capuzzi, in *Pathmarks*, ed. William McNeil (Cambridge: Cambridge University Press, 1998), 239–276; 259.

activity does not concern the plane of knowledge but that of praxis, which is treated synonymously with "practice," "action," "labor," "production" or "life" itself. In conceiving being as praxis, Schür-mann argues, Marx challenges the basic premise of metaphysics: "that being resides in theory."[16] Action appears, then, not as techno-metaphysical enframing, but as inherently manifold, and irreduc-ible to any theoretical foundation grounded in presence. Whence this discordance? Schürmann mentions several references for a transcendental interpretation of Marx, but in his own reading one of them stands out: Michel Henry's two volume work, *Marx*, pub-lished in 1976.[17] Given that Schürmann's lecture was delivered in 1977, we know that he read the book almost immediately upon its publication, and we may infer that he conceived this lecture course as an opportunity to work out his interpretation. Moreover, as is evident from the references in Schürmann's subsequent works, he closely followed the French debate around Henry's book after this lecture.[18] In response to a critical review of Henry's work by Paul Ricœur, Schürmann writes, in a footnote he included only in the English translation of *Le principe d'anarchie*: "Whatever the merits and shortcomings of Henry's transcendentalist picture of Marx may be, I am more concerned with the issues of metaphysical closure and plurification of the origin than with a literal interpretation of Marx."[19] One can, then, read his lecture as a forceful attempt to wrest a transcendental reading from the letter of Marx's text.

---

16 In this volume, 55.

17 Michel Henry, *Marx*, 2 vols. (Paris: Gallimard, 1976)/*Marx: A Philosophy of Human Reality*, trans. Kathleen Blamey McLaughlin (Bloomington: Indiana University Press, 1983). As for the other references, Schürmann names: Kostas Axelos, *Marx, penseur de la technique: De l'aliénation de l'homme à la conquête du monde* (Paris: Les Éditions de Minuit, 1961)/*Alienation, Praxis, and Techne in the Thought of Karl Marx*, trans. Ronald Bruzina (Austin: University of Texas Press, 1976); and Hans Staudinger, "Karl Marx als ökonomischer Transzendentalphilosoph," *Die neue Zeit* 39 (1921): 453–459. In contrast to Henry, Axelos and Staudinger do not understand praxis as individual or posit a radical heterogeneity of reality and ideality.

18 See Reiner Schürmann, "Anti-Humanism: Reflections of the Turn towards the Post-Modern Epoch," in this volume, 113 n. 48.

19 Schürmann, *Heidegger on Being and Acting: From Principles to Anarchy*, 321 n. 28. See Paul Ricœur, "Le 'Marx' de Michel Henry," *Esprit* 2:10 (1978): 124–39; also in his *Lectures*, vol. 2, *La contrée des philosophes* (Paris: Seuil, 1992), 265–293. The original

The singular place of Henry's *Marx* in the history of twentieth century philosophy is indicated by its reception. Largely ignored by French, let alone English, Italian or German Marxists, its seminal importance was acknowledged in the readings of Marx developed by Jacques Derrida and François Laruelle.[20] Schürmann's main interest in the work concerns Henry's thesis of an *"ontological heterogeneity of reality and ideality,"*[21] which Schürmann translates into the broader constellation of an an-archic fracture between being and action. One can gauge from this how important the engagement with this aspect of Henry's work—whom Schürmann had already cited in his very first book on Meister Eckhart, and from whom he would subsequently borrow the notion of "radical phenomenology"[22]—might have been in the development of his thinking leading to the publication of *Le principe d'anarchie*. The heterogeneity of reality and ideality is, according to Henry, the result of Marx's introduction of an entirely new notion of transcendental subjectivity that is no longer defined in relation to an object, as consciousness or intentionality. On the contrary, subjectivity is characterized as the self-affection of life in the individual experience of bodily needs, and as the actions that the individual undertakes to satisfy these needs.[23] Recast in this way, the transcendental subject excludes "all transcendence, all

---

French version references both Henry and Ricœur in the bibliography but does not contain this note. See *Le principe d'anarchie: Heidegger et la question de l'agir*, 439, 442.

20   See Jacques Derrida, *Spectres of Marx*, trans. Peggy Kamuf (London: Routledge, 2006), 234–237 n. 7; François Laruelle, *Introduction to Nonmarxism*, trans. Anthony Paul Smith (Minneapolis: Univocal, 2015), 43–44.

21   Henry, *Marx*, vol. 1, 41–42/*Marx*, 22.

22   Reiner Schürmann (1972), *Maître Eckhart ou la joie errante* (Paris: Éditions Payot & Rivages, 2005), 153. A revised and expanded version was published in English as *Wandering Joy: Meister Eckhart's Mystical Philosophy* (Great Barrington, MA: Lindisfarne, 2001), 89. Significantly, the reference to Henry concerns the question of univocity in Eckhart. For Schürmann's use of "radical phenomenology," see, for instance, Reiner Schürmann (1984), "Legislation-Transgression: Strategies and Counter-Strategies in the Transcendental Justification of Norms," in *Tomorrow the Manifold: Essays on Foucault, Anarchy, and the Singularization to Come*, ed. Malte Fabian Rauch and Nicolas Schneider (Zurich: Diaphanes, 2019), 77–120; 114–117.

23   This highly idiosyncratic notion of the subject as the auto-affection of life—strictly opposed to the metaphysical subject of representation—is at the center of Henry's thought. Henry situates this approach in the context of the post-structuralist deconstruction of the subject and against Heidegger's destruction of subjectivity in Michel Henry,

representation, it in fact cannot give itself in the exteriority of represented being."[24] This defines, for Schürmann, the radical immanence
of Marx's thought: "Reality—or being—is found in its total incapacity
to step beyond itself, that is, beyond need, hunger, suffering, work.
This radical immanence of reality is what Marx calls 'life'."[25] Being is
life, always singularized and localized by a mortal body.

This notion of transcendental subjectivity, Schürmann argues,
both exposes and exceeds the "humanism" implicit in metaphysics,
that is, its various reductions of being to an object to be grasped
and mastered by a subject: "The theoretical attitude has remained
the unchallenged horizon within which Western philosophy has proceeded. Subjectivity, within this horizon, was [...] the objectivity of
the object insofar as the object received its being from appearing
before such a subject."[26] By shifting the locus of transcendental genesis from theory to praxis, Marx's notion of the subject abolishes its
objective corollary and the entire apparatus of idealization, universalization, and representation. In contrast to Henry, who does not
use this terminology, Schürmann characterizes this as Marx's "nominalism," a term that denotes here the irreducibility of difference and
aims at highlighting how Marx responds to the oldest question of philosophy. For being, recast as subjective action, is irreducibly multiple
and, by virtue of this, resists objectification: "Philosophy is thus finished in as much as it means *theorein*, manifestation of an object."[27]
The 'grounding' of being in subjective praxis—always understood in
the irreducible plurality of singular and finite practices—disperses
the metaphysical notion of an origin grounded in presence: "There is
no origin, but only a profusion of originary actions by which individuals satisfy their basic needs."[28] Conceived as ontologically originary,
the activity of the Marxian subject is, therefore, "the first concept

---

"The Critique of the Subject," in *Who Comes after the Subject?*, ed. Eduardo Cadava,
Peter Connor and Jean-Luc Nancy (New York and London: Routledge, 1991), 157–167.

24   Henry, *Marx*, vol. 1, 377/*Marx*, 162.
25   In this volume, 87.
26   In this volume, 55.
27   In this volume, 53.
28   Schürmann, "Anti-Humanism," in this volume, 106.

that introduces multiplicity into being—and brings philosophy back to Democritus and Heraclitus."[29]

For Henry and Schürmann, the exegetical exigency consists in demonstrating that, in Marx, this "interpretation of being as production and as praxis" serves as the transcendental principle of genesis, whereas all social, economic, and historical categories are derivative of this principle.[30] Of particular importance for them are Marx's seemingly Kantian locutions, scattered across *The German Ideology*, of "living individuals" as the "premises" and "precondition" of history. As ontologically originary, the subjective praxis of "living individuals" is the condition of possibility for history, intersubjectivity, and economics, which are figured, phenomenologically, as exteriority and, theoretically, as abstractions and hypostases. Subjective praxis therefore functions as what Schürmann terms the "philosophical axis," determining and localizing all "regional" theories in Marx's work. This, of course, goes against the grain of almost all Marxist readings of Marx, since the premise is here always that social, economic, and historic circumstances are formative of the individual, not vice versa. The counterargument is not that such theories and their categorial apparatuses are illegitimate; but rather that they are derivative of subjective practice. If Henry polemicizes that "Marxism is the ensemble of misinterpretations that have been given of Marx," this is precisely because Marxism treats such categories as originary and in so doing restores the primacy of the universal that Marx had undone.[31]

The central target here is Louis Althusser, whose thesis concerning the "epistemological break" in Marx's work is harshly criticized.[32]

---

29 In this volume, 59.

30 Henry, *Marx*, vol. 1, 29/*Marx*, 13.

31 Ibid., 9/1. Translation modified.

32 See Louis Althusser, *For Marx*, trans. Ben Brewster (New York: Vintage, 1969), 32–38 and 223–241, on the presentation of the "epistemological break" and its "antihumanist" implications, respectively. On Althusser's critique of phenomenological readings, see, for instance: "Marxism cannot for one moment discover or rediscover itself along the path of this empiricism, whether it claims to be materialist or sublimates itself in an idealism of the ante-predicative, of the 'original ground' or of 'praxis' [...]. The concepts of origin, 'original ground,' genesis and mediation should be regarded as suspect *a priori* [...]." Louis Althusser et al. (1966), *Reading Capital*, trans. Ben Brewster (London: New Left Books, 1975), 63.

Yet, as far as Schürmann is concerned, this relation is particularly complex—and cannot be reduced to the opposition of structuralism and phenomenology—since he seeks both to retain Althusser's characterization of Marx's break with humanism in 1845 and to show how far Althusser is mistaken about the broader philosophical constellation that makes this break possible. Althusser, Schürmann argues, rightly dates and names Marx's achievement as a turn to "anti-humanism," yet his presentation "is a simplification precisely insofar as it labels this break 'epistemological'."[33] For in casting the break as epistemological, Althusser reinstates what Schürmann takes to be a realism of universals and obliterates the epochal constellation in which humanism is decentered. As we saw, for Schürmann, this is the closure of the metaphysical field, where the subject appears as the last in a series of strategies that ground action in a first philosophy.[34] While Althusser rightly registers the disappearance of man as philosophical foundation, the primacy he gives to the problem of epistemology prohibits him from recognizing the full implications of Marx's discovery: "Not a new method for science, but a displacement of the understanding of what reality is: precisely not graspable through universally valid rules and laws, but an always localized, finite, concrete effort to satisfy individual needs."[35] Ignorant of this irreducibility, Althusserian structuralism repeats the most metaphysical of maneuvers, insofar as it generates a privileged form of knowledge, based on universals, that pretends to ground, inform, and guide the action of the 'masses.' Moreover, Schürmann argues that this "break" in Marx's work is not as sudden as Althusser would have it; it rather follows a chiasmic movement, in which the primacy of universals reverts into a primacy of individuals after 1845.

---

33 Schürmann, "Anti-Humanism," in this volume, 101.
34 See Reiner Schürmann, "Modernity: The Last Epoch in A Closed History?," in *Tomorrow the Manifold*, 55–76.
35 In this volume, 43.

3. The concrete individual and social form

Schürmann's argument pivots on the contrast between Marx's philosophical axis and the Marxist use of his insights. Aside from 1960s French structuralism, Schürmann takes aim at what he terms "humanist Marxism," among which he counts various representatives of the Frankfurt School: Adorno and Horkheimer, Habermas, and Marcuse.[36] With regard to both the structuralist and humanist varieties of Marxism, Schürmann argues that they relapse into a realism of universals that Marx, with the philosophical shift articulated in *The German Ideology*, had overcome: according to this philosophical axis, the vantage point from which the destruction of the philosophy of consciousness and the corresponding history of ontology can be carried out is that of a realism of the concrete individual. On Schürmann's interpretation, which in its resonance with Dognin's and Henry's readings is conceived in contrast to Marxist doctrine, Marx's crucial achievement lies not in identifying the class antagonism as the driving force of history but in establishing the transcendental character of the individual's appropriation of the means for life. This specifically Marxian philosophy becomes eclipsed in the systematic and universalizing effort of Marxist theories of action. The elision, which is tantamount to a reversal of Marx's key contribution, is expressed not only in Althusser's analysis of the 1845 break in terms of a "continental shift" from one epistemology to another rather than from the epistemological a priori to a "practical a priori,"[37] but also in Marcuse's notions of a "negation

---

36 In this volume, 16–17. The reproach that Althusser retains a realism of universals in his structuralism resonates in many ways with recent discussions of Althusser's engagement with Spinoza. In fact, Althusser also proclaimed himself a nominalist, famously arguing that "nominalism" is *"the only conceivable materialism in the world."* Louis Althusser, "The Only Materialist Tradition," trans. Ted Stolze, in *The New Spinoza*, eds. Warren Montag and Ted Stolze (Minneapolis: University of Minnesota Press, 1997), 2–19; 10. On the more recent debates on Althusser's late Spinozism, especially with regard to "left Heideggerianism," see Katja Diefenbach, "Althusser with Deleuze: How to think Spinoza's immanent cause?," in *Encountering Althusser*, eds. Katja Diefenbach, Sara Farris et al. (London and New York: Bloomsbury, 2013), 165–184.
37 Schürmann, *Le principe d'anarchie*, 343–354/*Heidegger on Being and Acting*, 236–245.

of philosophy" and of the "great refusal."[38] On Schürmann's reading, the latter's insistence on contradiction and a dialectical concept of negation, in its narrowing down of the philosophical scope, formally anticipates the Althusserian epistemological reduction and loses sight of Marx's emphasis on the constitutive split that occurs within the laboring individual, replacing it with an opposition between constituted social forms. As a result, humanist Marxism mistakes Marx's critique of a historically specific form of philosophy for a negation of philosophy altogether.[39]

To illustrate how humanist Marxism reproduces the philosophy of representation that Marx had overcome, Schürmann cites Marcuse's claim, from *Reason and Revolution*, that "Marx's early writings are not philosophical [but] express the negation of philosophy."[40] For Marcuse, the negation of philosophy comes with "an indictment of the totality of the existing order."[41] Negation, as the driving power of dialectical thought, has a liberating function that constitutes it as a positive act reinstating "that-which-is-not" as

---

38   In this volume, 17.

39 ́ While in these lectures, Marcuse acts as a stand-in for the Frankfurt School in general, Schürmann occasionally refers to other representatives of this 'school' in more detail across his work. Jürgen Habermas and Karl-Otto Apel are mentioned frequently throughout the notes to *Heidegger on Being and Acting*. On Adorno and Horkheimer, see *Heidegger on Being and Acting*, 368–369 n. 47 (this note is not included in the French edition, see *Le principe d'anarchie*, 311) and *Des hégémonies brisées* (Zurich and Berlin: Diaphanes, 2017), 420 n. 10/*Broken Hegemonies*, trans. Reginald Lilly (Bloomington and Indianapolis: Indiana University Press, 2003), 662–663 n. 10. On Schürmann's account, what distinguishes all these approaches from Heidegger's is their shared normative intent: "This premise of the 'history of being,' that there exists no primordial norm-giving order, marks the radical difference between Heidegger and the Frankfurt School. One of the preoccupations that indeed makes a 'school' out of this latter group is its attempt to construe forms of ultimate legitimation [...]" (*Heidegger on Being and Acting*, 318 n. 13; this note is not included in the French edition, see *Le principe d'anarchie*, 54). It is not necessary to specifically note that the monolithic representation of these thinkers under the heading of Frankfurt School drowns out important differences between them, but see the correspondence of Marcuse and Adorno on the student movement in 1969, Herbert Marcuse and Theodor W. Adorno, "Correspondence on the German Student Movement," trans. Esther Leslie, *New Left Review* 233 (1999): 123–136.

40   In this volume, 21; Marcuse, *Reason and Revolution*, 258.

41   Marcuse, *Reason and Revolution*, 258.

part of that reality from which "that-which-is" repels it, and therefore is the precondition for overcoming a reality that represses "its own real possibilities."[42] However, the problem with this dialectical idea of negation, Schürmann argues, is that it rests on a *representation* of society as constituted by contradictory social forms. These contradictions are conceived starting from the idea of man as 'generic being,' that is, from the point of view of a realism of universals: individual men trying to universalize themselves. What is lost in this perspective is the "double meaning of man" that subtends Marx's writings during the period in which he establishes the laboring individual as the transcendental or "originary site of truth."[43] Anticipating a motif that would become central to his later work on the double bind,[44] Schürmann emphasizes the discordant aspects of this transcendental materialism: on one hand, it establishes the laboring individual as a principle or *primum captum* that, transposed into the social form of the class, comes to orient the Marxist theories of action. Turned against this universalization, on the other hand, there remains the surplus of a truly singular and concrete activity, the moment of a specific actualization of individual life. Dialectical negation can only be applied to a reality already constituted as a principle, even if this reality is grasped as contradictory. What Marx actually negates, then, is philosophy as a philosophy of principles that pushes for "the abstract realization of the totality" of generic being and that underpins the Hegelian concept of negativity.[45] In the realism of the concrete individual, labor is not a mere "process of objectivation" but the "concrete realization of [the] attributes in each man."[46]

By elaborating this distinction between Marxian philosophy and Marxist doctrine, Schürmann aims to provide reference points for the

---

42 Herbert Marcuse, "A Note on Dialectic," in *The Essential Frankfurt School Reader*, ed. Andrew Arato and Eike Gebhardt (New York: Continuum, 1977), 444–451; 447.

43 In this volume, 37, 23.

44 See Reiner Schürmann, "Ultimate Double Binds," in *Tomorrow the Manifold*, 121–149.

45 In this volume, 37.

46 In this volume, 37.

"phenomenological destruction of Marx's ontology"[47] that Heidegger
had not undertaken, a destruction that is meant to philosophically
clear the perspective upon the concrete practice of the individual,
by releasing it from its subsumption under universal foundations. If
practice is thus turned into the an-archic focus for philosophy, critical
weight is placed on the notion of the *concrete*, which guarantees the
irreducible multiplicity of the origin or ground of individual practice.
It is precisely this guarantee that Marcuse, who in the late 1920s had
collaborated with Heidegger and had explored a phenomenology of
historical materialism based on "the concrete ground of historicity"[48]
laid out in *Being and Time*, challenges when he accuses Heidegger
of promulgating a "false concreteness."[49] Schürmann takes up this
charge in *Heidegger on Being and Acting*, suggesting that it indicates
a gap that Heidegger had indeed left unthought, but which in no way
affects that which Heidegger had thought. On Schürmann's view,
Marcuse's humanist Marxism cannot fill this lacuna precisely because
it re-establishes a realism of universals and thus fails to emerge from
"the slumber of thoughtlessness."[50] Only if Marxian philosophy is
seen as a historically specific destruction of metaphysical principles
rather than as a negation of all philosophy can its vitalist moment fill
the gap left by Heidegger.

---

47   In this volume, 22. Schürmann adds that there are "only nine allusions to Marx
in Heidegger's works." Despite the few explicit references, many of Heidegger's later
essays—"Kant's Thesis About Being," for instance—betray the crucial role of Marx
and Marxism as antagonists to and interlocutors of Heidegger's project. See Martin Heidegger, "Kants These über das Sein," in *Wegmarken, Gesamtausgabe*, vol. 9,
445–480/"Kant's Thesis about Being," in *Pathmarks*, 337–363.
48   Herbert Marcuse, "Contributions to a Phenomenology of Historical Materialism,"
in *Heideggerian Marxism*, ed. Richard Wolin and John Abromeit (Lincoln and London: University of Nebraska Press, 2005), 1–33; 10.
49   Herbert Marcuse, "Heidegger's Politics: An Interview," in *Heideggerian Marxism*,
165–175; 166. Schürmann notes (in this volume, 17) that Marcuse, in *Eros and Civilization* (Boston: Beacon Press, 1966), 149–150, borrows the notion of "great refusal" from
Alfred North Whitehead's *Science and the Modern World* (New York: Pelican Mentor,
1948), 159. Similarly, Marcuse's reference to "false concreteness" in this interview is
reminiscent of Whitehead's critique of the "fallacy of misplaced concreteness" that
haunts modern science when it accidentally mistakes "the abstract for the concrete"
(ibid., 52).
50   Schürmann, *Le principe d'anarchie*, 354/*Heidegger on Being and Acting*, 245.

Schürmann counters the loss of the equivocity between the Marxist ontology of universals and Marx's philosophy of the concrete individual by historicizing what, in humanist Marxism, remains a metaphysical negation: the Marxian axis does not negate philosophy as such, but rather that specific form of philosophy that rests on an epistemological a priori. From the ruins of this philosophy, Schürmann recovers the discordant ground that gives rise to both universalizing totality and individual activity. In Marx, Schürmann finds an an-archic philosophy of life as "moving subjectivity"[51] that he positions against the archic reactivation driving traditional Marxisms. If individual practice produces "transcendental history,"[52] the temporality that is operative here is indexed to the particular human being. There is, however, another temporality, a historical time that imposes itself on the individual epochally, and the heterogeneity of which complicates the transcendental subject's constitutive activity.

Schürmann's philosophical interest remains firmly located in the bifurcation brought about by Marx between the representation of 'universal man' and the transcendental individual. The duplication of the notion of 'man' indicates what Marx calls a *"fundamental division"*[53] that permeates the individual in its historical situation. This division retrieves the double bind between the history-making capacity of the individual and its subjection to the heteronomy of historical time. Equivocity is the very condition of the historical place in which the individual finds itself and, by virtue of this, any negation of philosophy is a historically specific negation, which Schürmann elsewhere grasps through the notion of the "historial differend."[54] Its specificity derives not only from the specific form of philosophy that it targets, but from its subversion of the historical time to which it finds itself subjected. In that sense, it does not effect a negation of philosophy *tout court*, but an abolition of

---

51   In this volume, 18.
52   In this volume, 24.
53   Karl Marx, *Zur Kritik der Hegelschen Rechtsphilosophie*, in *Marx-Engels-Werke*, vol. 1 (Berlin: Dietz Verlag, 1981), 281/*Critique of Hegel's Philosophy of the State*, in *Marx/Engels Collected Works*, vol. 3 (London: Lawrence & Wishart, 1975), 77. The phrase Marx uses is *"wesentliche Diremption."*
54   Schürmann, *Des hégémonies brisées/Broken Hegemonies*, volume 2, chapter 5.

first philosophy: the materialist dialectic must not, as in traditional Marxism, "be turned into a *prima philosophia* (not to say, an ontology), its foremost aim is to liquidate the idea of *prima philosophia* and to replace it with an *ultima philosophia.*"[55] Not a first, but an ultimate philosophy that prepares the diremption of the false identity between the universal and the individual.

4. Remarks on this edition

The present volume is based on a 72-page typescript for the lecture course "Reading Marx," which Reiner Schürmann held at the New School for Social Research in the fall of 1977. To reflect the orientation of Schürmann's reading, the subtitle "On Transcendental Materialism" has been added to Schürmann's original title. Our general editorial approach has been to intervene silently in all non-ambivalent cases, to tacitly correct obvious mistakes in page references, as well as to reinstate italics in citations that Schürmann did not himself render. In a few places, where several subsequent references to the same pages occur within a single paragraph, we have merged them into one. Wherever we have made conjectures that are more than grammatical, we have added a note indicating our changes. Those editorial endnotes are placed in square brackets. The few substantial editorial interventions in the body of the texts, as well as, in the table of contents, those sections crossed out by Schürmann by hand,[56] are marked by angle brackets (‹›). Schürmann's interpolations within citations are marked with square brackets and the initials "—R.S." A notable feature of the original typescript is that the first twenty pages are heavily annotated by hand, whereas the remaining pages have mostly typed marginalia. Lastly, the typescript includes two drawn diagrams with typed legends, which are here rendered in a digitized form.[57]

---

55 Theodor W. Adorno in a letter to Alfred Sohn-Rethel from November 3, 1936, in Theodor W. Adorno and Alfred Sohn-Rethel, *Briefwechsel. 1936–1969*, ed. Christoph Gödde (Munich: edition text + kritik, 1991), 10–11.
56 See Lecture 1.c and Lecture 7.4.
57 We would like to thank Katharine Wimett for the graphic rendering.

Schürmann cites from various editions of Marx's works, referring both to German editions and to English translations. In many cases, Schürmann rearranges cited sentences, omitting words and whole phrases that would interfere with readability, without always indicating it. We have retained these changes uncommented where they do not significantly modify the meaning of the original, and have added notes giving the original passages where they do. Beyond this, we have unified the citation system, referring wherever possible to the most accessible editions of the collected works of Marx and Engels, the *Marx-Engels-Werke* in German and the *Marx Engels Collected Works* in English. Abbreviations have been written out in full, and foreign terms as well as Schürmann's underlines have been italicized (a typographical option not available to Schürmann). In the case of the numerous references to Michel Henry, we have inserted the page references to the two volumes, which in the typescript appear in the margin, into the text body.

In accordance with Schürmann's own handwritten suggestion on the last page of the lecture typescript, the nine sessions of the lecture course are followed by Schürmann's essay on "Anti-Humanism." Concluding this volume, we append the plan of the course given to the students at the beginning, the divergence of which with the actual structure of the course is worth noting. Thus, while the initial plan outlines fourteen sections grouped into four parts, the typescript only has nine lectures, each of which is divided into several subsections. Only two of the sections given in the initial plan (4, 12) appear in a similar form in the typescript (4.1, 8.2), with the remaining sections not directly corresponding to the plan in any way. This divergence marks the ongoing nature of Schürmann's grappling with Marx's place in his topology of broken hegemonies.

Plan of the Course

I. Introduction

    1. Reading Marx: the problem of homogeneity in the texts.

II. 'Humanism' and the Epistemological Break
('Manuscripts of 1844')

    2. The critique of alienations.

    3. The concept of subjectivity in the early Marx.

    4. The critique of subjectivity and the epistemological break.

III. Marx's Transcendentalism
('German Ideology' and 'Poverty of Philosophy')

    5. The foundation of history.

    6. The foundation of social relations.

    7. The foundation of economy.

    8. Marx's transcendentalism and the critique of consciousness.

    9. The first break with philosophy of consciousness:
       the refutation of the ontology of sense reality.

    10. The second break with philosophy of consciousness:
       the refutation of "theory."

    11. The transcendental status of "practice."

IV. The Concept of Ideology

    12. The proportionality "reality : representation :: reality : irreality."

    13. Reality as foundation of representation ("it is not consciousness which determines life, but life which determines consciousness").

    14. The universality of labor versus the universality of theoretical categories.

Two papers are required: 1) a short text analysis (maximum 7 pages) of a text of the student's choice, due November 10; 2) a term paper the topic of which must be related to the course and must be approved by the instructor (maximum length 12 pages).

Tentative Chronology of Reiner Schürmann's Courses at the New School for Social Research

Year	Term	Course Title	All Instances
1975	Summer	*Nietzsche and the Problem of Truth* [The Philosophy of Nietzsche]	*1975, Summer* *1977, Fall* *1984, Spring* *1988, Spring*
	Fall	*Augustine's Philosophy of Language* [Augustine's Philosophy of Mind]	*1975, Fall* *1979, Fall* *1984, Fall* *1991, Fall*
		Aristotelian & Neoplatonic Elements in Late Medieval Philosophy [Medieval Neoplatonism and Aristotelianism]	*1975, Fall* *1981, Spring* *1987, Spring*
		Karl Jaspers' Philosophy of Existence	*1975, Fall* *1979, Spring*
1976	Spring	*Plotinus –* *A Study of the Enneads with Particular Emphasis on En. IV and VI* [Plotinus—The Philosophy of Plotinus]	*1976, Spring* *1978, Fall* *1983, Fall* *1988, Fall* *1992, Fall*
		The Scope of Hermeneutics [Hermeneutics]	*1976, Spring* *1979, Fall* *1986, Fall*
	Fall	*The Contemporary Crisis in the Philosophy of Man* [Philosophical Anthropology II: Its Contemporary Crisis]*	*1976, Fall** *1981, Spring* *1990, Spring*
		*Medieval Philosophy I: Neoplatonism**	*1976, Fall** *1979, Spring* *1980, Fall (ver. II)* *1990, Spring (ver. I)*

Year	Term	Course Title	All Instances
1977	Spring	*Heidegger's Destruction of Metaphysics** [The Phenomenology of the Later Heidegger]	1977, Spring* 1980, Spring 1984, Fall 1994, Spring †
		Kant's Critique of Pure Reason – Part II*	1977, Spring 1980, Spring 1988, Spring 1988 Fall
	Fall	*Reading Marx*	1977, Fall
		The Philosophy of Nietzsche [The Philosophy of Nietzsche]	1975, Summer 1977, Fall 1984, Spring 1988, Spring
		Medieval Concepts of Being	1977, Fall 1982, Fall
1978	Spring	*Medieval Philosophy II:* *Neo-Aristotelianism* *(13th–14th centuries)*	1978, Spring 1991, Spring
		Heidegger as an Interpreter of Kant	1978, Spring 1985, Spring 1991, Spring
	Fall	*The Philosophy of Plotinus* [Plotinus—The Philosophy of Plotinus]	1976, Spring 1978, Fall 1983, Fall 1988, Fall 1992, Fall
		Contemporary French Philosophy [From Transcendentalism to "Post-Structuralism"; Systems and Breaks: Foucault and Derrida †]	1978, Fall 1983, Spring 1994, Spring †
		Heidegger's Being and Time*	1978, Fall* 1982, Spring 1986, Fall 1993, Spring

Year	Term	Course Title	All Instances
1979	Spring	*Medieval Philosophy I: Neoplatonism*	<u>1976, Fall</u>* 1979, Spring <u>1980, Fall (ver. II)</u> <u>1990, Spring (ver. I)</u>
		Karl Jaspers' Philosophy of Existence	1975, Fall <u>1979, Spring</u>
		*Kant's Practical Philosophy***	1979, Spring**
	Fall	*Augustine's Philosophy of Mind* *[Augustine's Philosophy of Language]*	1975, Fall 1979, Fall 1984, Fall <u>1991, Fall</u>
		Kant's Critique of Pure Reason – Part I	<u>1979, Fall</u>, <u>1982, Fall</u> 1987, Fall <u>1988, Spring</u>*
		Hermeneutics *[The Scope of Hermeneutics]*	<u>1976, Spring</u> <u>1979, Fall</u> <u>1986, Fall</u>

Year	Term	Course Title	All Instances
1980	Spring	Kant's Critique of Pure Reason – Part II	1977, Spring* 1980, Spring 1988, Spring 1988, Fall
		The Phenomenology of the Later Heidegger [Heidegger's Destruction of Metaphysics]	1977, Spring 1980, Spring 1984, Fall 1994, Spring †
	Fall	Medieval Philosophy I: Neoplatonism (ver. II)	1976, Fall* 1979, Spring 1980, Fall (ver. II) 1990, Spring (ver. I)
		Modern Philosophies of the Will	1980, Fall 1987, Spring 1992, Spring
		Philosophical Anthropology	1980, Fall 1989, Spring
1981	Spring	Aristotelian & Neoplatonic Elements in Late Medieval Philosophy [Medieval Neoplatonism and Aristotelianism]	1975, Fall 1981, Spring 1987, Spring
		The Contemporary Crisis in the Philosophy of Man [Philosophical Anthropology II: Its Contemporary Crisis]	1976, Fall* 1981, Spring 1990, Spring

Year	Term	Course Title	All Instances
1982	Spring	Kant's Political Philosophy	_1982, Spring_ _1992, Fall_
		Heidegger's Being and Time	_1978, Fall*_ _1982, Spring_ _1986, Fall_ _1993, Spring_
		Seminar in Methodological Problems [X-listed Econ J323s; co-taught with Prof. R. L. Heilbroner]	_1982, Spring_
	Fall	Medieval Concepts of Being	_1977, Fall_ _1982, Fall_
		Kant's Critique of Pure Reason – Part I	_1979, Fall,_ _1982, Fall_ _1987, Fall_ _1988, Spring*_
1983	Spring	From Transcendentalism to "Post-Structuralism" [Contemporary French Philosophy; Systems and Breaks: Foucault and Derrida †]	_1978, Fall_ _1983, Spring_ 1994, Spring †
	Fall	The Philosophy of Plotinus [Plotinus – A Study of the Enneads with Particular Emphasis on En. IV and VI; Plotinus]	1976, Spring _1978, Fall_ 1983, Fall 1988, Fall _1992, Fall_
		Kant's Critique of Judgment	_1983, Fall_ _1990, Spring_

Year	Term	Course Title	All Instances
1984	Spring	*Medieval Practical Philosophy* [Latin Metaphysics of Nature]	*1984, Spring* *1988, Spring*
		The Philosophy of Nietzsche [Nietzsche and the Problem of Truth]	1975, Summer *1977, Fall* 1984, Spring *1988, Spring*
	Fall	*Augustine's Philosophy of Mind* [Augustine's Philosophy of Language]	1975, Fall 1979, Fall 1984, Fall *1991, Fall*
		Heidegger's Destruction of Metaphysics [The Phenomenology of the Later Heidegger]	1977, Spring* *1980, Spring* 1984, Fall 1994, Spring †
1985	Spring	*Greek and Latin Philosophies of Time*	*1985 Spring* *1989, Spring*
		Heidegger as an Interpreter of Kant	*1978, Spring* 1985, Spring 1991, Spring
1986	Fall	*Hermeneutics* [The Scope of Hermeneutics]	*1976, Spring* *1979, Fall* *1986, Fall*
		Heidegger's Being and Time	*1978, Fall* *1982, Spring* *1986, Fall* *1993, Spring*
		Parmenides	*1986, Fall* *1991, Fall*

Year	Term	Course Title	All Instances
1987	Spring	*Medieval Neoplatonism and Aristotelianism* [Aristotelian & Neoplatonic Elements in Late Medieval Philosophy]	1975, Fall 1981, Spring 1987, Spring
		Modern Philosophies of the Will	1980, Fall 1987, Spring 1992, Spring
	Fall	*Kant's Critique of Pure Reason – Part I*	1979, Fall 1982, Fall 1987, Fall 1988, Spring*
1988	Spring	*Latin Metaphysics of Nature* [Medieval Practical Philosophy]	1984, Spring 1988, Spring
		The Philosophy of Nietzsche [Nietzsche and the Problem of Truth]	1975, Summer 1977, Fall 1984, Spring 1988, Spring
		Kant's Critique of Pure Reason – Part I	1979, Fall, 1982, Fall 1987, Fall 1988, Spring*
		Kant's Critique of Pure Reason – Part II	1977, Spring 1980, Spring 1988, Spring 1988, Fall
	Fall	*Plotinus* [The Philosophy of Plotinus; Plotinus—A Study of the Enneads with Particular Emphasis on En. IV and VI]	1976, Spring 1978, Fall 1983, Fall 1988, Fall 1992, Fall
		Kant's Critique of Pure Reason – Part II	1977, Spring* 1980, Spring 1988, Spring 1988, Fall

Year	Term	Course Title	All Instances
1989	Spring	*Greek and Latin Philosophies of Time*	1985, Spring 1989, Spring
		Philosophical Anthropology: An Introduction	1980, Fall 1989, Spring
	Fall	*Heidegger's Thinking in the 30s*	1989, Fall
1990	Spring	*Medieval Philosophy I (Neoplatonism; version I)*	1976, Fall* 1979, Spring 1980, Fall (ver. II) 1990, Spring (ver. I)
		Kant's Critique of Judgment	1983, Fall 1990, Spring
		Seminar on Philosophical Anthropology II: Its Contemporary Crisis [The Contemporary Crisis in the Philosophy of Man]	1976, Fall* 1981, Spring 1990, Spring
1991	Spring	*Medieval Philosophy II: Neo-Aristotelianism (13th–14th centuries)*	1978, Spring 1991, Spring
		Seminar on Heidegger as an Interpreter of Kant	1978, Spring 1985, Spring 1991, Spring
	Fall	*Parmenides*	1986, Fall 1991, Fall
		Augustine's Philosophy of Mind [Augustine's Philosophy of Language]	1975, Fall 1979, Fall 1984, Fall 1991, Fall

Year	Term	Course Title	All Instances
1992	Spring	*Luther:* *The Origin of Modern Self-consciousness*	<u>1992, Spring</u>
		Modern Philosophies of the Will	<u>1980, Fall;</u> 1987, Spring <u>1992, Spring</u>
	Fall	*Kant's Political Philosophy*	<u>1982, Spring</u> <u>1992, Fall</u>
		Plotinus [*The Philosophy of Plotinus;* *Plotinus—A Study of the Enneads* *with Particular Emphasis on En. IV and VI*]	1976, Spring 1978, Fall 1983, Fall 1988, Fall 1992, Fall
1993	Spring	*Heidegger's Being and Time*	<u>1978, Fall*</u> <u>1982, Spring</u> <u>1986, Fall</u> <u>1993, Spring</u>
		Meister Eckhart	<u>1993, Spring</u>
1994 †	Spring †	*Heidegger's 'Destruction of Metaphysics'* † [*The Phenomenology of the Later Heidegger*]	1977, Spring* <u>1980, Spring</u> 1984, Fall 1994, Spring †
		Systems and Breaks: *Foucault and Derrida* † [*Contemporary French Philosophy;* *From Transcendentalism to "Post-Structuralism"*]	<u>1978, Fall</u> <u>1983, Spring;</u> 1994, Spring †

The *Chronology* is based on the NSSR Bulletin and cross-referenced with the Lecture Notes

— the underlined years/terms—e.g. <u>1980, Spring</u>—are the ones mentioned in the Lecture Notes
— * = Course *is not* mentioned in the NSSR Bulletin although Lecture Notes, with specific years/terms, have been found
— ** = Course *is* mentioned in the NSSR Bulletin but *no* Lecture Notes linked to the former have been found
— [ ] = alternative title for different years/terms
— † = Course *is* mentioned in the NSSR Bulletin but was never taught due to death.

Lecture Notes of Reiner Schürmann at the NSSR—
Pierre Adler's Inventory (1994)

Volume I: Ancient Philosophy	Volume II: Medieval Philosophy	Volume III: Early Modern Philosophy
• Parmenides • Greek and Latin Philosophies of Time • The Philosophy of Plotinus • Augustine's Philosophy of Mind • Medieval Practical Philosophy	• Medieval Philosophy I: Neoplatonism • Medieval Philosophy I: Neoplatonism Version II • Medieval Philosophy II: Neo-Aristotelianism (13th/14th centuries) • Medieval Concepts of Being • Aristotelian and Neo-Platonic Elements in Late Medieval Philosophy • Meister Eckhart	• Luther: The Origin of Modern Self-consciousness • Kant's *Critique of Pure Reason* Part I • Kant's *Critique of Pure Reason* Part II • Kant's *Critique of Judgment*

Volume IV: Philosophy in Modernity	Volume V: Heidegger	Volume VI: 20th Century Philosophy
• Kant's Political Philosophy • Reading Marx • The Philosophy of Nietzsche • Modern Philosophies of Will • Karl Jaspers' Philosophy of Existence	• Heidegger's *Being and Time* • Heidegger's Destruction of Metaphysics • Heidegger as an Interpreter of Kant • Heidegger's Thinking in the 1930s	• Hermeneutics • Philosophical Anthropology • Philosophical Anthropology II, Its Contemporary Crisis • Methodology of Social Sciences (co-taught with Prof Heilbroner) • Contemporary French Philosophy

Reiner Schürmann
Selected Writings and Lecture Notes

Edited by
Francesco Guercio, Michael Heitz,
Malte Fabian Rauch, and Nicolas Schneider

This edition aims to provide a broader perspective on the prolific, multifaceted, and still largely unrecognized body of work produced by Reiner Schürmann (1941–1993). It brings together a selection of Schürmann's as yet unpublished lecture notes, written for the courses he delivered at the New School for Social Research in New York between 1975 and 1993, with previously uncollected essays.

These works offer an additional avenue into the repertoire already available—including recent re-editions of his major philosophical works and of his only novel. The printed works will be complemented by a digital edition of Schürmann's typescripts, along with transcriptions and an extensive critical apparatus.

We hope that the *Selected Writings and Lecture Notes* will contribute to a renewed appreciation of the scope of Schürmann's philosophical endeavor and help to establish him as one of those thinkers who are indispensable for the understanding of our present—or, rather, to show our present as the moment of legibility for Schürmann's work. We are grateful to the Reiner Schürmann Estate for entrusting us with the responsibility of this work and for their full endorsement.